P9-EJU-921

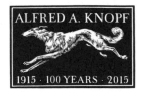

NINE ESSENTIAL THINGS
I'VE LEARNED ABOUT LIFE

Nine Essential Things
I've Learned About Life

HAROLD S. KUSHNER

ALFRED A. KNOPF   NEW YORK   2015

THIS IS A BORZOI BOOK
PUBLISHED BY ALFRED A. KNOPF

www.aaknopf.com

Knopf, Borzoi Books, and the colophon are registered trademarks of
Penguin Random House LLC.

Library of Congress Cataloging-in-Publication Data
Kushner, Harold S., author
Nine essential things I've learned about life / Harold S. Kushner.
        pages   cm
    "This is a Borzoi book"—Title page verso.
    ISBN 978-0-385-35409-7 (hardcover)—
        ISBN 978-0-385-35410-3 (eBook)
  1. Self-actualization (Psychology)—Religious aspects—Judaism.
2. God (Judaism).   3. Jewish way of life.   4. Spiritual life—Judaism.
                I. Title.
        BM729.S44K87 2015
    296.7—dc23   2014049740

Jacket design by Stephanie Ross

Manufactured in the United States of America
First Edition

For Suzette,
who has made the good times more joyous and
the hard times more bearable over so many years

Contents

Contents

Preface

This book is in part a memoir, a description of the path I followed from adolescence to a career as a rabbi, and of the challenge my wife and I faced when our son was diagnosed with an incurable illness. It is also the story of how organized religion, in all of its branches and formulations, has changed over the course of my lifetime. The religion I teach and practice is very different from the religion I was taught. I blame no one for this change except perhaps the calendar. I was born in 1935. Most of my teachers at rabbinical school had been born in the nineteenth century. Most of my congregants were born in the last third of the twentieth century, and many of their children in the twenty-first. Rethinking religion and theology to address the spiritual needs of that generation has been the defining issue of my rabbinate and underlies much of what I write about in this book.

The credit for much of what is best about this book goes to my editor at Alfred A. Knopf, Jonathan Segal, with whom I have worked on several previous books. He helped me understand what this book should be about and guided me through the process of articulating it. He pointed me toward several key themes and steered me away from more than one blind alley.

A heartfelt word of thanks also to Peter L. Ginsberg of Curtis Brown Ltd. Peter has been with me for almost all of my books, and I would not have been able to write them without his efforts.

I am also deeply grateful to my wife, Suzette, to whom I have dedicated the book, for her encouragement early and late, and for the time and effort she put into reading the manuscript and calling my attention to matters large and small that needed to be changed.

And above all, I am grateful to the Source of all my spiritual insight and understanding, for giving me the ability to recognize where people hurt and giving me the language to ease their pain.

HAROLD S. KUSHNER
Natick, Massachusetts

NINE ESSENTIAL THINGS
I'VE LEARNED ABOUT LIFE

CHAPTER ONE

Lessons Learned Along the Way

*In the twenty-first century, the religious agenda will be set
not by tradition's answers but by congregants' questions.*

For thirty years, I had the perfect job. I was a congregational rabbi. I studied, I taught, I officiated at life-cycle events—bar mitzvah services, weddings, and funerals—trying to enhance the joy and mitigate the sorrow of those moments with my words and with elements of the Jewish tradition, all things I had been taught to do and felt good about doing. (I confess there was one other aspect of being a congregational rabbi that pleased me. I have read that the most frightening thing a person can contemplate, even more than the fear of death, is the fear of having to speak in public. That's not me. In a room where two hundred people are sitting and listening and one person is standing and speaking, I will always be most comfortable being the one standing and speaking.)

I'm not sure how I ended up being a rabbi. It was never my intention growing up. I don't think it ever occurred to me, nor to my parents, who suggested regularly that they would like me to be a doctor. I entered college with no idea of what I would do professionally, hoping that college would give me a direction. My father was a successful businessman, which ruled that out as a career. I did not want to go into business and fail, disappointing my father, nor did I want to go into business and be more successful than my father (a highly unlikely outcome). I have known families in which that engendered not pride but resentment.

I entered Columbia in 1951, listing my major as "liberal arts," which left open all possibilities short of medical school. I also took advantage of Columbia's proximity to the Jewish Theological Seminary, where my mother had studied to be a Hebrew teacher some twenty-five years earlier and where some of her most revered teachers still taught. The Seminary offered evening classes for students who wanted the education without seeking a career in Jewish professional life.

In those evening classes, I came to recognize four or five familiar faces from my freshman classes at Columbia, and we bonded. We would come back from class and stay up late talking theology, trying to make sense of the Holocaust, details of which had just become widely known, and discussing what the State of Israel, founded just a few years earlier, would mean for Jewish life. Several of those friends were planning to study for the rabbinate, though none of them did. Only I ended up there. After graduating from Columbia in 1955, I enrolled in the Seminary's rabbinical school and emerged five years later as a Conservative rabbi.

My spiritual life—what I believe, teach, and practice—has been shaped in large measure by two sets of circumstances. The first was the home I grew up in and the synagogue my family and I attended. The rabbi at the Brooklyn Jewish Center was Israel Levinthal, recognized as one of the outstanding preachers of the American Jewish community. Stories circulated of how Orthodox Jews would walk over the Williamsburg Bridge from the Lower East Side to Brooklyn on Friday nights (as they could not take trains on the Sabbath) to hear Levinthal speak. The quip was that every newly ordained Conservative rabbi would head out to his first pulpit with two books in his luggage: the pocket guide to Jewish practice and the collected sermons of Israel Levinthal. To this day, I cannot sit down to write a sermon without feeling Rabbi Levinthal's presence looking over my shoulder to make sure I am being faithful to the text.

I would describe the religion practiced in my home as "observant but not compulsive." When we lit the Sabbath candles on a Friday night or observed the traditional dietary rules about permitted and forbidden foods, I never had the sense that we were obeying a command from a God who would be displeased with us if we had not done those things, nor did we obsess about the consequences of our inadvertently making a mistake. Rather, we felt we were making a statement about who we were as a family and, although I don't think the word would have occurred to any of us, we were bringing a measure of holiness into an ordinary middle-class home, turning mundane moments into appointments with God. I could not have predicted at the time that the concept of "observant but not compulsive" and the absence of a belief in a God who would punish us for disobedience would go on to become cornerstones of my personal and professional life.

The second circumstance that shaped my religious outlook was the illness and death of our son, Aaron, from one of the world's rarest diseases, progeria, the "rapid-aging" syndrome, as I chronicled in my book *When Bad Things Happen to Good People*. It was in the presence of my sick and dying child that I discovered how inadequate the traditional perspective was that I had grown up with and had been taught, that God has His reasons, which we cannot comprehend or judge. It neither made sense of the suffering nor offered us much in the way of comfort. If I was to continue to serve as a rabbi and to honor my son's memory, I would have to find a better explanation.

I think of the first circumstance, the religion of my childhood home and synagogue, as "religion done well," religion fashioning a community and introducing moments of specialness into an ordinary home. And I think of the second as my encounter with "religion done badly," more concerned with protecting God's reputation than with helping worshippers in need. The notion that an all-wise, all-powerful God who is totally good must have had His reasons for inflicting incurable illness on innocent children, reasons beyond the comprehension of a human mind or soul, was worse than unhelpful. It was offensive, saying to us either "You must have done something to deserve this" or "In times to come, you will understand why this was the right thing to happen to you." I heard this from many people after my book came out: "Now you know why God did this to your child, so that you would write this book that would help millions." I'm sorry, but I choose to believe that any God worth worshipping would say, "I really don't need you to be My press agent. I need you to bring solace and comfort to My bleeding children on earth."

More than anything else, my half century of congregational service and my dozen or so books have been dedicated to reformulating that traditional theology. I've done this not to protect God from bad theologians and people's righteous anger, but to rescue people who need God from having to choose between a cruel God and no God at all.

I heard a story some years ago about a couple celebrating their twentieth wedding anniversary by going out to dinner at a fancy restaurant. Leaving the restaurant, they got into their car to drive home. The wife turned to the husband and said, "What's happened to us over the years? Do you remember when we were courting, when we were first married, how we would get into the car and snuggle up close to each other, and drive somewhere holding on to each other? Now look how far apart we're sitting." And the husband responded by pointing to the steering wheel and saying, "I haven't moved."

For many of us, there was a time when we were young when we felt close to God. We had been taught that God loved us and was watching over us, and that made us feel safe. We tried to be worthy of God's love and were troubled by guilt every time we told a lie or took something that didn't belong to us. When we learned of other people's suffering, as when my best friend died of a brain tumor when he was ten years old, we fell back on the assumption that God knows what is best for us better than we do. That childhood faith did not last. War, crime, serious illnesses affecting people we cared about, the emerging truth about the Holocaust, and the inevitable disappointments of life cost us that simple faith of our childhood, and like the wife in the story, we found ourselves feeling distant from the God to whom we had once felt so close but now found unreliable. I hope that this book, born out of my own struggles with faith lost and recovered, will help to close that gap, to let us know that God has not moved but that we have come to see Him more clearly.

My years at rabbinical school were an extraordinary intellectual feast. For four years (plus a year of independent study in Israel), I was confronted on a daily, if not hourly, basis by great minds, great scholars, men who dominated (and in some cases had created) their areas of expertise. I had the privilege three times a week of watching the mind of Saul Lieberman analyze a puzzling page of the Talmud. I was introduced to a new level of biblical scholarship, at once critical and reverent. And I met the man who would change my life, Mordecai Kaplan. Where my other professors had answers to text-related questions, Professor Kaplan had questions to challenge the answers we brought to class. He accomplished the Copernican revolution of moving the center of gravity in religion from divinely ordained observances to the collective will of the community. Judaism was what serious Jews did, not what books described them as doing. Christianity would be defined by how Christians acted today, not by what medieval scholars wrote long ago. In the process of teaching me, he prepared me for the crisis that would arise from the one serious flaw in my otherwise excellent rabbinic education. More about that later.

I was ordained a rabbi in June 1960. We graduates were expected to give two years of service before we began our careers, in some position that would otherwise not be able to have a rabbi: a small congregation, an organization serving the less fortunate, or the military chaplaincy. I made myself available to the chaplaincy. This country had been very good to my family, welcoming my parents when they immigrated from Lithuania, educating my brother and me, sending an army to defeat the Nazis before they could finish the destruction of European Jewry, and I felt I owed it something for that. As a clergyman, I was exempt from the draft, so I had to go to court and have the exemption waived. I was commissioned a first lieutenant and, with my new bride of a few months, headed out to Fort Sill in Lawton, Oklahoma.

It was in many ways a good experience. I had time to study. Every Monday, I would meet for lunch with the post psychiatrist, who was a member of my congregation there. He taught me how to understand and respond to the problems the GIs brought to me on a daily basis. And as a colleague of mine put it, as a new rabbi I got to make my rookie mistakes on congregants who did not have the power to fire me.

I completed my two-year obligation, served a four-year apprenticeship in a major Long Island synagogue, and in the summer of 1966 assumed the pulpit of Temple Israel in the Boston suburb of Natick. Soon enough, I discovered the strengths and the weaknesses of my seminary training.

After years of intensive study of classical texts, I

left school full of answers. The implicit message of my rabbinical school was: "These answers are the essence of Judaism. If your congregants ask you questions to which these answers don't fit, educate them to ask more appropriate questions." Some of that worked. The meaning and emotional impact of the customs and usages of traditional Judaism can be magical, and I trust this holds true for other religions as well. Done right, they can transform a moment from ordinary to sublime. A wedding ceremony can be elevated from a mundane legal procedure to a celebration of the miracle of love and commitment, a human being entrusting his or her happiness to the care of another human being, giving parents and grandparents a glimpse into the promise of vicarious immortality. A bar mitzvah service done right (how often does that happen?) can be more than an elaborate birthday party. It can celebrate a child's crossing the threshold, being publicly recognized as an incipient adult, capable of mastering the skills required of adults in his community. A funeral is not simply the disposal of a dead body. It represents the gathering of the community to provide comfort to the bereaved in time-honored, time-tested ways, so that the mourner need not feel abandoned at a time when he or she is most prone to feeling abandoned.

Congregants did come to me with questions, but most of their questions were not the ones my seminary training had prepared me for. I knew which prayers are recited at the Sabbath service, but I had no ready answer for the congregant who said to me, "Saturday is the busiest day in my business. That's when I make most of the money to pay the bills at home. What right do you have to tell me to skip work and come to services instead?" Or the parents who said to me, "Little League baseball is the most important thing in our eleven-year-old son's life right now. If the temple makes Junior Congregation mandatory, we'll pull him out of Hebrew school before we take him out of Little League." (My answer: we'll see him in Junior Congregation when Little League season ends.)

My Seminary education made me an authority on the Jewish dietary laws. I had a three-page printout of which fish had fins and scales and could be eaten by observant Jews, and which fish lacked them and were nonkosher. But I was rarely asked about that. I was more likely to be asked, "Why do I have to restrict what I serve my family today based on which foods were not good to eat in the heat of the Sinai desert?"

Those encounters taught me the first rule of religious life in the twenty-first century and what made it different from religious life in previous times. The agenda for religion today will be set not by yesterday's answers but by today's questions. I still believe there is great wisdom in yesterday's answers. Human nature has not changed that much. But my rabbinic education, splendid as it was, saw congregants as passive consumers of ancient and eternal truths. To be religious was to obey, not necessarily to understand, and certainly not to question. That perspective did not prepare me for a world in which the meaning of words like "commitment," the structure of the family, issues of religious identity in an open society, and the respective roles of men and women were in flux. Those changes set in motion major changes in the way Jews and Christians alike responded to their respective religious traditions. Sociologists have identified the salient difference between working-class and middle-class people as a function of how much control someone has over his or her life. Working-class people, as well as women in premodern times, were accustomed to following orders, deferring to authority. By contrast, middle-class and upper-class people understand that it is not their obedience but their judgment that people look to them for. They feel they have not only the right but the obligation to question the way things have always been done. Citing a verse from Leviticus to justify the exclusion of gays or pointing to a thousand years of precedent to undergird priestly celibacy is no longer a persuasive argument.

My job as a rabbi was neither simply to perform nor to inform, but to transform. Sometimes that meant trying to change the behavior of a congregant to embrace time-tested values, and sometimes it meant changing the observance, peeling away its ancient outer shell so that the message at its core could more easily emerge.

Arthur Hertzberg, a historian, posited a theory as to why American Jewish immigrants were so ready to dispense with practices that had been part of Jewish life for centuries. He asked: "During the great waves of immigration from Eastern Europe between 1881 and 1924, which East European Jews were most likely to emigrate and which ones were more likely to stay behind?" For the most part, he speculated, it was the young, the more ambitious, the ones for whom Jewish life in Europe had less to offer who boarded the ships. The more learned, the rabbis and scholars, were more likely to stay behind. As a result, we ended up with a large Jewish population with a strong sense of Jewish identity but few religious leaders and very little serious knowledge of the history and reasons for what Jews traditionally did. For them, Jewish life was a mix of vaguely remembered holiday customs and Polish superstitions. The message they passed on to their children was "This is what Jews do. Don't ask me why, or what it means. We just do it."

My job called on me to listen carefully to what my congregants were saying, sometimes to pierce the veil of anger or mockery in which they phrased their questions, and to try to hear the faint echo of a soul yearning for a meaningful relationship to God if it could be presented to them in terms that they could intellectually and morally respect. The woman who could not see the need to mourn for her recently deceased unloved father, a man who had left his wife and ignored his children, was not really telling me that she had no need to grieve. She was saying, whether she realized it or not, that mourning for the man who had given her life and then rejected her was going to be a complicated process and she didn't know where to start. She had strong but confused feelings, and she was asking for my help in sorting those feelings out, even if she didn't understand that that was what she was doing. I would have betrayed the trust of congregants who informed me that they would not mourn their father because they were not religiously inclined had I not warned them that this was not just a matter of obeying or ignoring the rules of Judaism. You cannot shrug off the loss of a parent the way you can shrug off the loss of a movie you never got around to seeing. It was my duty to warn them not that God would think less of them if they broke one of Judaism's rules, but that those rules were forged by human beings who understood the human soul, and that every hour they saved this week by not formally grieving they would pay back with interest in a therapist's office.

Measured by the scale I have discussed here, the congregants in my synagogue come in three flavors. There are those, may God bless them and may their tribe increase, who love their religion and can't get enough of it. They take classes, attend services, staff committees, volunteer to bring meals to shut-ins, and are always looking for ways to make things better. They do it not in the expectation that God will think more kindly of them but because they like themselves better when they do those things. Then there are those who show up only for major services and the occasional family bar mitzvah. (I wonder if there is any other aspect of their lives where they ask how little they can get for what it costs.) But perhaps the most interesting ones are the people who challenge me, not as a kind of game ("let's see if we can stump the rabbi") but out of a genuine willingness to learn. They have found that religion as it has been presented to them throughout their lives is unworthy of either their intellectual respect or their emotional attachment. Their implicit deal with me is that they will take their religion more seriously if I can show them not how old and time-tested it is but where it can answer their most profound questions, questions about relationships, about life's unfairness, about right and wrong, about revenge and forgiveness, and about the meaning and purpose of their lives. Nobody at school told me that this would be my challenge, but hardly a day has passed since then without my confronting it. That was the flaw in my rabbinic education. When I was ordained a rabbi at age twenty-five, they told me I was ready to go forth and teach. The truth was, I was at best ready to go forth and learn.

CHAPTER TWO

God Is Not a Man Who Lives in the Sky

I came to my pulpit in Natick prepared to take on the role of Defender of the Faith. I knew I would be interacting with congregants who would challenge me on the credibility of biblical stories and the relevance of Jewish observances, and I was prepared to try to convince them. But some of the most frustrating encounters came when I was approached by a teenager whose first words to me were "I don't believe in God." The young man would say that as a challenge ("I don't believe in God and I dare you to convince me that I am wrong"), but less confrontational seekers sometimes said the same as a genuine question ("I'd like to be able to believe in God, but how can I when I read about some of the things that go on in the world?"). Typically, the skepticism could be traced to one of two factors: the impact of having someone close to him die, often after a pain-filled, lingering illness, or the enormity of the Holocaust, making it hard for him to believe that God was in charge of this all too often cruel world.

I would share with the young man the usual "proofs" for God's existence—the argument from design, the Unmoved Mover, and so on—but I don't think I ever convinced him, or anyone else for that matter. If anything, I probably made things worse. "If a rabbi can't make a better case than that for God's existence," I was once told, "I guess there is no persuasive case. It's all wishful thinking."

Then one day, an astute colleague shared with me a tactic he uses, one that apparently can be traced to the great Protestant preacher Harry Emerson Fosdick. Instead of arguing with his young congregant and hoping to change his mind, he would say to him, "Tell me about this God you don't believe in. There are a lot of gods I don't believe in. Maybe we'll discover that we both reject the same notion of God, and then maybe we can find an understanding of God that we can both accept."

I don't believe that God is a person who lives in the sky. For that matter, even to speak of God as "He" misrepresents what I believe, but I am a prisoner of the English language, which lacks a neutral pronoun. (I refuse to speak of God as "it.") I can only fall back on the excuse that God, in biblical Hebrew, is grammatically male but functionally both male and female—sometimes a stern, demanding Father-God, sometimes an embracing, comforting, nourishing Mother-God.

I am attracted to the suggestion of a grammarian (I wish I could remember his name) that "she" will always refer to an exclusively feminine subject, but "he" may not point to a specifically male one. He suggests that "he" can refer to a member of a population of mixed or indeterminate gender, while "she" is reserved for a specifically female subject (even as Eve was carved from the body of an androgynous Adam to fashion a specifically female creature). A grammatically male God could refer to a divine entity that embraced both polarities of gender, while a grammatically female deity would always be a goddess.

We have a soap dish in our bathroom at home that reproduces the scene from Michelangelo's painting of the Sistine Chapel, the moment when God reaches out to touch Adam and bring him to life. It portrays God as a muscular man with gray hair and a long white beard. It's great art but bad theology. I believe that we lose more than we gain when we give people a visual image of God to hold on to. It makes God real and accessible to them at the cost of giving them misleading theological information about God's nature.

When I undertook the task of editing *Etz Hayyim,* the commentary to the Torah for the Conservative movement, the first demand of the advisory committee the movement provided me with was that we write a gender-free commentary when it came to talking about God. I told them, "I'm not sure I can do that. I agree with your goal, but I'm not about to write a sentence like, Here God tells God's people that God will punish them if they reject God's demands." But they insisted, and we managed to forge a commentary that said everything we wanted to say without referring to God as "He" and without doing violence to the English language.

Once, at a conference, I was asked which of the Ten Commandments was the hardest to obey. In retrospect, I suspect the best answer would have been the fifth, the one about honoring one's parents. I think it's probably impossible for someone to go through adolescence and never get into a nasty dispute with one's parents or do something that embarrasses them. But the answer I gave was the second, about not making a graven image of God, which we usually think of as the easiest to avoid. Who worships idols these days? But that's not what the commandment is about. It tells us not to represent God in human (or for that matter, animal) form, the way Michelangelo does on our soap dish. "Don't make a graven image of God" means "don't portray God as a thing."

Early in my rabbinic career, when I was younger and had an easier rapport with young children, I would sometimes go into one of the classrooms of our religious school and have a discussion with the ten- and eleven-year-old children about God. I would say to them, "If I asked you to draw a picture of God, what would your picture look like?" Typically, one youngster would come up with something straight out of Michelangelo: "God is a wise old man with a long beard and gray hair." Another might say, "God is a tall man with a black beard and He wears a *kippah*" (a head covering worn by pious Jewish men).

After a few more suggestions along those lines, I would say, "Those are very interesting ideas, but there was one answer I thought somebody might give me but nobody did. I thought that maybe when I asked you to draw a picture of God, somebody might say, 'We're not supposed to.' After all," I went on, pointing to a list of the Ten Commandments on the classroom wall, "isn't that one of the Ten Commandments, not to make an image of God? Why do you think we have that commandment? Is it because the picture wouldn't turn out nice enough and God's feelings would be hurt?

"I don't think so. I think it's because God is not a person like us, who lives in the sky. God is real, but God is real in a very different way than you and I are real. If we have a picture of God as a man, does that mean that God is a man and not a woman, and that men are more similar to God than women are? If God in your picture is old, should you worry that God might not understand the problems that you face as a young person? If God in your picture has white skin, should a child with black or brown skin, or an Asian child, feel that he or she is less close to God than white-skinned, blue-eyed children?"

Because our minds can only work in concrete terms, because it's hard to think about something abstract, we inevitably think of God the way we think of people, even as we try to remind ourselves that that is not accurate. The story is told of the little girl who asked her mother, "Does God have skin?" The mother, who had some sophisticated ideas about religion, answered her, "No, dear, God doesn't have skin." The little girl giggled and said, "He must look funny without it."

The medieval Jewish philosopher Maimonides had perhaps the best solution when he wrote that God has no physical form, but because we humans can only think in physical terms, we picture God as a person. We speak about our prayers reaching the ears of God, we hope that our deeds are pleasing in the eyes of God, we tell the Passover story of how the hand of God smote the Egyptians. Maimonides warns us that that kind of thinking about God is inevitable, but even as we engage in it, we have to remind ourselves that it is our limitation, not the reality of God, that leads to that kind of concrete thinking and speaking.

To picture God is to define Him, and to define Him is to limit Him. That's what a definition does: it includes some things and rules everything else out. To presume to define God comes across as saying that we know everything there is to know about God. I would rather have us believe and say that the effort to understand what God can mean in our lives is an ongoing, never-ending one. It should teach us to approach the idea of God in a spirit of humility.

The notion that God is there to do what we need or expect Him to is what angered God in chapter 32 of Exodus, the story of the Golden Calf. After the Revelation at Mount Sinai, Moses went up the mountain to receive the words of the Ten Commandments from God Himself. Moses stayed up there so long that the Israelites felt abandoned. It was Moses who had introduced them to God, told them what God demanded of them and what He offered them in return. He had been the visible embodiment of God's concern for the people. He was their link to God. So they persuaded his brother, Aaron, to build them a statue of a bull (an image of formidable strength and power, though the Bible belittles it by calling it a calf) to represent God's continuing presence in their midst. That caused God to be angry with them. Days after promising not to make an image of God, they had given in to the human weakness of not believing in anything they couldn't see. But a God we could see would be a limited God. That God would have some characteristics, but their specificity would rule out His having others.

To fashion a viable representation of God is inevitably to identify certain traits—masculinity, youth or age, strength—as divine and suggest that their opposites are less so.

When I proclaim, "The Lord is one," as I do daily in my prayers, I'm not making a mathematical statement. It is not a report of the population of divine beings in heaven. It is a theological statement. It is not, as many people take it to be, a denial of the religious significance of other putative divine beings: God is God and they are not. It is the insistence that God embraces all polarities, male and female, young and old, scolding and forgiving. Everything—all polarities—finds its place in God. "God is one" means something like "God is all."

There is a passage in chapter 17 of Genesis in which God changes the name of the ancestor of the Israelites. "You shall no longer be called Abram, but your name shall be Abraham" (Genesis 17:5). Some Bible scholars see that as the reconciliation of two Semitic dialects. Several traditional commentators relate it to the Hebrew word "*hamon*," which means "multitude," in light of what God goes on to say later in the verse: "I will make you the father of a multitude of nations." The most common explanation is that the letter *H* (the letter *heh* in Hebrew) is an abbreviation of the sacred Name of God, YHWH, and the name change is the equivalent of God's "branding" Abraham as belonging to Him.

I would suggest another possible explanation. In Hebrew, the letter *H* is often used to signify the grammatically feminine. One changes a verb or noun from masculine to feminine by adding an *H*. In the Genesis narrative before God changes Abraham's name, Abraham comes across as an insensitive, uncaring husband. Twice, when famine drives Abraham and his wife Sarah and their flocks into dangerous neighborhoods looking for pasture, Abraham represents Sarah as his sister, not his wife, so that the local ruler will feel free to take her into his harem without having to kill Abraham first (Genesis 12:10–13 and again in 20:1–7). Only after the *H* is added does Abraham become a caring husband, and only then are he and Sarah able to have a child together. It may be that adding the *H* to his name put Abraham in touch with his feminine side, helping him to become a more complete human being and preparing him for the responsibilities of parenthood and his role as the founder of a new faith. He has achieved some of the wholeness, the embrace of polarities, that his newfound God stands for.

"Tell me about the God you don't believe in; maybe I don't believe in Him either." I don't believe that "God" is another name for Santa Claus, that He knows who has been naughty and who has been nice and grants or denies our fondest wishes accordingly. The country music singer Garth Brooks had a hit song some years back titled "Unanswered Prayers." In it, he tells of a man who goes to a communal event and sees a woman of about his own age whom he realizes he had a crush on in high school. Every night he would go to bed praying to God to make her love him as he loved her, not understanding why God would not grant the heartfelt wish of a pious teenage boy. Now, all these years later, seeing who he has grown up to be and who she has grown up to be, he comes to the conclusion that "some of God's greatest gifts are unanswered prayers."

I thought it was a lovely song but terrible theology. I don't buy into the tactic of making bad news acceptable by insisting that God knows what's best for us better than we do. That may work for a high school youngster with a crush on someone in his math class, but what about the parent praying for a cure for a sick child? What about the unemployed man praying for a chance to earn a living? I have known many people who tried to bargain with God. They prayed for something and reminded God of their many virtues, from charity to church or synagogue attendance. (Where did we get the idea that attending church or synagogue was a favor we were doing God for which God owed us something?) Sometimes they got what they hoped for and were quick to thank God for it. Most of the time, though, they were left either upset with themselves for not deserving the prize or upset with God for withholding the outcome they felt they deserved.

Generally, I have a "live and let live" attitude toward other people's theology. If it works for them, who am I to deprive them of a cherished belief? How can I be certain that I'm right and they're wrong? But I remember one time when I lost all respect for someone because of what that person expounded about God.

Our son, Aaron, attended a private Jewish day school affiliated with the Conservative movement. Not only did we want him to have a more intensive religious education and environment, but we also thought that a small school that emphasized academic excellence over athletics would be a better fit for Aaron, given his physical limitations. It worked out very well, except for one time.

When Aaron was in second or third grade, we noticed that he was suddenly treating his younger sister more kindly. He was also frequently asking if there was anything he could do around the house to be helpful. He was even more diligent than usual about his studies and about religious services at school. From time to time, he would ask me questions about what it meant to be good, what good behavior consisted of. We were puzzled by his behavior but had no reason to question it.

After a few weeks, Aaron suddenly became depressed and sad. Once or twice, we heard him cry himself to sleep. Then the truth came out. One of his teachers, whose notions of God and prayer were more extreme than those of the rest of the faculty, had told the class that if there was something they really wanted very badly and if they were very good, following all the rules of the Torah, and prayed hard for that thing, God would grant their wish. Aaron tried so hard to be good, and we suspect he was praying to God to make him normal, like other children. When it didn't happen, he became deeply disillusioned with prayer, religion, and religious services.

As far as I am concerned, a person is free to believe anything he or she wants to about the efficacy of prayer. But to tantalize a child with an incurable medical condition with the hope that an exemplary life will lead to God's answering his prayer is an unforgivable act of wanton cruelty.

You may remember that there was an experiment in 2006 to see whether prayer would help sick people heal faster. A large cohort of postoperative patients, matched for severity of illness and discomfort, was divided into three equal parts. One group was prayed for by people who believed in the power of prayer to invoke God's healing grace, and the people were informed that they were being prayed for. A second group was similarly prayed for but not told about it. And a third group was not prayed for at all. There was no discernible difference in the speed or quality of their recovery.

CNN interviewed me shortly after the results were announced and asked, "Doesn't that prove that prayer is an ineffective waste of time and effort?" I told the interviewer, "It doesn't prove a thing. It isn't God's job to make sick people healthy. That's the doctors' job. God's job is to make sick people brave, and in my experience, that's something God does really well."

Prayer, as I understand it, is not a matter of begging or bargaining. It is the act of inviting God into our lives so that, with God's help, we will be strong enough to resist temptation and resilient enough not to be destroyed by life's unfairness.

I am sometimes asked, Do you believe in a personal God, a God who knows who I am and what I'm dealing with? Does God know that it's me who is asking Him for something? Or is He an impersonal force, like gravity? I don't believe that God recognizes me as Harold, the Conservative rabbi from Massachusetts who had a son who died. But neither do I conceive of God as an impersonal force like gravity or magnetism. To me, God is like love, affecting all people but affecting each one differently, according to who he or she is. God is like courage, a single trait but one that manifests itself differently as it is filtered through the lives and souls of specific individuals.

The truth is, life is unfair, and we would do well to come to terms with that fact. Boorish people are blessed with athletic or musical skills that qualify them to earn more money in a year than many of us will earn in our lifetime. Saintly people are struck down by disease before they can use their gifts to help others. The task of religion is not to teach us to bow our heads and accept

God's inscrutable will. It is to help us find the resources to live meaningfully and to go on believing, even in a world where people often don't get what they deserve.

How would our understanding of God and religion change if we could think of the term "God" as a verb rather than as a noun? (Grammatically, the Hebrew label of God, YHWH, resembles a verb form more than a noun.) "God" would not refer to a divine actor who makes or does not make certain things happen. "God" would mean that in certain moments, certain things would happen that testified to the presence and activity of God. God would be present in the moment, not in the activity, and our question would no longer be "Where was God?" but "When is God?" Illness would be the result of Nature, but healing would testify to a moment of God's presence.

Think of it this way: no scientist has ever seen an electron, but all scientists agree that electrons exist. No physicist has ever seen a quark, but all physicists believe that quarks are real. Why? Because when they look into their microscopes, they see things happening that could only happen if quarks and electrons existed. I believe in the reality of God the way scientists believe in the reality of electrons. I see things happening that would not happen unless there is a God.

The liberal theologian Jim Wallis was a speaker at the Stanford University Baccalaureate on June 12, 2004. He stated, "When I was growing up in my Christian world, I was told the greatest battle of our time is between belief and secularism, but I now believe that the real battle is . . . between cynicism and hope." Religion can teach us not to despair. Sometimes the good guys do win—not always, to be sure, but just often enough to let us hold on to hope.

I don't believe in a God who treats human beings like puppets, pulling our strings to make us do things, or a God who spends His mornings deciding who shall live and who shall die, let alone who will win a high school football game.

I don't believe in a God who creates us with certain weaknesses and passions, making us vulnerable to greed, lust, and temptation, and then punishes us for not being perfect, for giving in to those temptations, or, in some theologies, condemns us for even thinking about forbidden things, a God for whom bad thoughts are as sinful as bad deeds. If you don't like how susceptible human beings are to lust and selfishness, don't blame the people. Complain to the Manufacturer.

We can aspire to be better tomorrow than we were yesterday, more charitable with our time, money, and attitude. But the challenges of being human, being the only living creatures whose lives are not totally guided by instinct, are so many and so complex that nobody can get through life, nobody can get through a single day, without doing something wrong—not necessarily illegal or wicked, but not the perfect choice. If I can understand that flaw when I look at my own life and the lives of those around me, I would like to think that God understands it as well.

I don't believe in a God who is so emotionally needy that He can be bribed by flattery or blind obedience. There is a delightful Hasidic story about Mendel the tailor, who goes to his rabbi with a problem. He tells the rabbi, "I try to be the best tailor I can be. If a customer says to me, 'Mendel, you're a wonderful tailor; you're the best,' that makes me feel good. But if somebody came into my shop every day and told me, 'Mendel, you're a wonderful tailor,' or if a hundred people crowded into my shop to tell me that, it would drive me crazy. I wouldn't be able to get my work done. So my question is, does God really need to have every Jew in the world tell Him three times a day how wonderful He is? Doesn't He sometimes find it tedious?"

The rabbi answers him, "Mendel, that's a really good question. You have no idea how tedious it is for God to hear our praises all day, every day. But God understands how important it is for us to remind ourselves of all He does for us, so in His infinite kindness, He puts up with our incessant praying and accepts our praise."

The God I believe in is not so insecure that He holds it against people who doubt His existence, nor is He so eager to punish that He condemns people to Hell for errors of heart, mind, or faith. I read the Reverend Jonathan Edwards's famous 1741 sermon "Sinners in the Hands of an Angry God," in which he refers to "the God that holds you over the pit of hell, much as one holds a spider, or some loathsome insect over a fire . . . look[ing] upon you as worthy of nothing else, but to be cast into the fire." I hear similar sentiments from some present-day evangelists who delight in conjuring up the eternal punishment awaiting all who don't believe what they believe, and I find myself unable to recognize what they are advocating as religion.

Some years ago, I participated in an interfaith panel on Larry King's television program. The evangelical pastor on the panel told me that he respected me as an honest and caring person, but because I did not believe what he believed, I would not be saved but would be sent to Hell after I died. I responded, "You mean I get to spend eternity with Einstein, Gandhi, and Freud, and not with you?"

I cannot believe in, let alone worship, a God so given over to sadistic torture for people who displease Him that He would even invent Hell. As one Protestant minister of my acquaintance put it, "I believe that Hell exists, because my Bible tells me it does. But I also believe that God is so loving and forgiving that if there is a Hell, it is perpetually uninhabited."

The God I believe in is under no obligation to be the kind of God we would like Him to be, or even the kind of God we need Him to be. Begging Him, bargaining with Him, even living by His mandates will not cause the rain to fall and give us an abundant harvest, nor will it cure our disease or help us win the lottery. God's role is not to make our lives easier, to make the hard things go away, or to do them for us. God's role is to give us the vision to know what we need to do, to bless us with the qualities of soul that we will need in order to do them ourselves, no matter how hard they may be, and to accompany us on that journey.

CHAPTER THREE

God Does Not Send the Problem; God Sends Us the Strength to Deal with the Problem

There is a painting at the Museum of Fine Arts in Boston that fascinates me. When I visit the museum, I have trouble tearing myself away from looking at it. Between visits, I look at a postcard-sized replica of it on my desk and, in our basement, at a larger version of it, cardboard mounted, that years ago was a gift to our daughter to decorate her college dorm room. The original is a medium-sized painting, just thirty inches high and forty-eight inches across. It was painted in 1885 by the American artist Winslow Homer and is called *The Fog Warning*. It could serve as the cover illustration for Hemingway's novella *The Old Man and the Sea*. The work shows a lone fisherman in a rowboat with a large fish he has caught, struggling to return to his ship before a gathering fog envelops him. To me, Homer's painting proves the existence of God.

I don't find God, as many people do, in the beauty and orderliness of nature, the change of seasons, autumn in New England. How can I, with a straight face, ask the survivors of Hurricane Katrina in New Orleans, or Superstorm Sandy in New Jersey, or victims of the tsunami in Thailand to recognize God's presence in nature unless I believe in a capricious God unconcerned with the well-being of His creatures? If I celebrate God as the source of recovery from illness, must I also recognize Him as the source of injury, disease, birth defects?

On the first anniversary of Hurricane Katrina, I was invited to speak at an interfaith congregation in the largest church still standing in New Orleans's Lower Ninth Ward. I took as my text a passage from the first book of Kings, chapter 19. Things have become so bad in the land of Israel under the rule of the spineless King Ahab and the wicked Queen Jezebel that the prophet Elijah, in despair, runs away to the desert, to Mount Sinai, to reconnect with the God of Israel, the God of the Exodus and the Ten Commandments. We read, "There was a great and mighty wind, splitting mountains and shattering rocks, but the Lord was not in the wind. After the wind, an earthquake, but the Lord was not in the earthquake. After the earthquake, a fire, but the Lord was not in the fire. And after the fire, a still, small voice" (verses 11–12). The voice tells Elijah to go back to Israel and work to make things better.

"Did you hear that?" I asked the congregation packed into the church. "God was not in the wind, God was not in the fire. Where was God? His was the still, small voice inspiring your neighbors to go out in their rowboats to rescue people from their rooftops. God's was the still, small voice moving thousands of college students to spend their spring break mopping the streets of New Orleans instead of partying on a beach in Fort Lauderdale. God's is the still, small voice that will give you and your neighbors the courage and the determination to rebuild what was once and will again be one of America's great cities."

I recognize God as portrayed in the pages of the Bible, but even as I do so, I see the biblical narratives as refracted through the fallible personalities of the human beings who wrote the stories down thousands of years ago. There are parts of the Bible that I have no trouble accepting at face value. For example, King David died and was succeeded by his son Solomon. There are other pages I believe are meant to be taken seriously but not literally. The story of the Creation of the world, found in the opening pages of Genesis, is important, not because it tells us how long it took God to make a world (144 hours) but because it tells us what kind of world God made: an orderly world, filled with plants and living creatures capable of reproducing themselves, and with the emergence of human beings as the culmination of the creative process. Like many of the passages in the Bible, the Creation story is a myth, by which I do not mean a made-up story. In her 2009 book *The Case for God,* the scholar of religion Karen Armstrong defines a myth as "something that may or may not have happened once, but in a sense, happens all the time." The Creation myth comes to tell us something about the world we live in.

Are the narratives of the Bible true? Rabbi Jonathan Sacks, former chief rabbi of the Orthodox communities of the British Commonwealth, distinguishes not between truth and falsehood but between left-brain and right-brain truth. He writes in *The Great Partnership* (2012) about

the human mind and its ability to do two quite different things. One is the ability to break things down into their constituent parts and see how they mesh and interact. The other is the ability to join things together so that they tell a story. . . . The best example of the first is science, of the second, religion. Science takes things apart to see how they work. Religion puts things together to see what they mean. . . . The first is a predominantly left-brain activity, the second is associated with the right brain.

Our left brains tell us how the world is; our right brains offer us a vision of how the world might be.

Sacks goes on to suggest that when we use our left brain to make a point, we articulate a theory, moving from point to point in logical sequence from premise to conclusion. Once you concede the truth of the premise, you have no choice but to accept the truth of the conclusion. When we use our right hemisphere, the intuitive rather than the logical side of our brain, we don't set forth an argument. We tell a story. A story is true or false, not depending on whether it portrays the world as it is or has been but depending on whether it elicits an emotional response of "yes, that's how life works." Greek philosophy, and the heritage of Aristotle that dominates the scientific mind to this day, is unrelentingly left-brain. There is no room for emotion in it. The medical researcher who falsifies the results of an experiment because he so passionately wants his proposed cure for cancer to be effective is committing a fundamental sin, violating the canons of scientific research. Biblical theology is just as strongly right-brain, offering us a vision of the world not as it is but as it might be.

I have asked dozens of my Christian friends and students if they can remember their first introduction to the New Testament. Virtually all of them, Protestant and Catholic, young and old, pious and skeptical, told me the same thing. They were enchanted by the Gospels and could quote some of their favorite parables by heart.

But when it came to the Epistles of Paul and others, they felt they had stepped from the shallow water into the deepest part of the pool. They could never be sure what Paul was talking about.

Both kinds of thinking, left-brain and right-brain, will give you truth, but they will be very different kinds of truth. The prominent theologian Harvey Cox put it this way in *The Future of Faith* (2009): "In entering the Greek world, Plato's turf, the early Christians mixed biblical ideas into a Greek framework that often distorted their original meaning."

(The astute reader will notice what I have just done. To make my point about left-brain and right-brain thinking, I first cited the dictionary definitions, but then I told a story about conversations with Christian friends. I offered narrative rather than logical argument, as the Hebrew Bible and the Gospels do. Which mode did you find more persuasive?)

Sacks concludes his analysis in *The Great Partnership* by writing, "God lives in the right hemisphere of the brain, in empathy and interpersonal understanding, in relationships etched with the charisma of grace, not subject and object, command and control, domination and submission."

There are passages in the Bible that reflect a morality that was probably advanced for its time but that has been superseded by human evolution: the humane treatment of slaves (who, in biblical Israel, were not the property of their master, like the slaves in *Uncle Tom's Cabin,* but rather people whom economic difficulty had forced to sell their labor to a master for a period of seven years), the limited public role of women, and others. There are pages in the Bible in which prophets and psalmists pray for bloodthirsty vengeance against the nations that had ravaged their land—utterly understandable but not very edifying as a page of sacred Scripture.

In the world of the Bible, it made sense (that is to say, it was a right-brain truth) to believe that God was in full control of the world, that everything that happened in life happened because God wanted it to, and if it didn't make sense to us, the appropriate response was not to fashion a theology that would explain it but to perform an act of love and trust and accept what happened as God's will. "I don't like it and I don't understand it, but I have to believe that God knows what He is doing." In that world, the words of Job, "Shall we accept the good from God and not accept the bad?" (Job 2:10), were an appropriate way of responding to misfortune.

This was the case when, in 586 BCE, the Babylonians invaded the land of Judea, sacked Jerusalem, destroyed Solomon's Temple, and exiled the Judeans to Babylonia. That should have been the end of the Jewish people, as it was the end of the Ammonites, Moabites, and Edomites who were similarly conquered and exiled. The man who saved Judaism, and made Christianity possible, was the prophet Jeremiah.

Jeremiah lived in what was probably the most traumatic period in all of the Hebrew Bible. Before the war, he warned the people that God would not long tolerate their oppression of the weak and vulnerable, that a nation that did not deserve to survive would not long survive. Nobody believed him. They were supremely confident that God would let no harm come to the building that bore His name. But when the calamity came, Jeremiah was too loyal a Jew and too devoted to God to take any satisfaction in being proven right. He told the people that this had happened to them not because the Babylonian army was mightier than their army, which would have been a left-brain truth, and certainly not because the Babylonian gods were mightier than the God of Israel, but because the people had strayed from God's ways. That was the message that the Israelites needed to hear. Instead of assimilating into the majority culture, they learned to worship the God of their forefathers in exile, to "sing unto the Lord in a strange land."

When the accumulated injustices of life became too much for the theology of "God knows what He is doing" to accommodate, Jews and Christians alike turned to the idea of a World to Come where all the grievances of this life would be made up for.

Seeing suffering as God's will made it easier for people in authority to assume that their enemies were God's enemies as well, and to feel that they were doing God's will by mistreating them. In the nineteenth century, churchgoing slave owners convinced themselves that they were doing God's will by treating African American slaves as less than fully human, assuming on the basis of no evidence whatsoever that God's curse on Noah's son Canaan in Genesis 9:25, "he shall be a slave to his brothers," referred to people kidnapped from Africa. In the classic Western movie *The Magnificent Seven,* the bandit leader justifies his robbing the poor peasants of a nearby village by saying, "If God did not want them to be sheared, why did He make them sheep?"

Where, then, do I find God? I find God in the quiet heroism of Winslow Homer's fisherman, stretching to the limits of human strength and endurance to do what life calls on him to do. I find God in the willingness of so many people to do the right thing, even when the right thing is difficult, expensive, or unappreciated, and to reject the wrong thing no matter how tempting or profitable.

Where does an ordinary person find that willpower unless God is present, motivating that person to surpass himself? I find God not in the tests that life imposes on us but in the ability of ordinary people to rise to the challenge, to find within themselves qualities of soul, qualities of courage they did not know they had until the day they needed them. God does not send the problem, the illness, the accident, the hurricane, and God does not take them away when we find the right words and rituals with which to beseech Him. Rather, God sends us strength and determination of which we did not believe ourselves capable, so that we can deal with, or live with, problems that no one can make go away.

Let me tell you about the day I learned what it means to be a rabbi. I had been called to the home of a congregational family in which the husband and father had suddenly died of a heart attack. When I arrived, the grieving widow's first words to me were "Why would God do this to such a good man?" I tried to share with her my understanding of God's role in misfortune, my notion of a God who was good and kind but not all-powerful, but I could see that my words were not helping her. On the contrary, her eyes glazed over as I offered my theology. It was at that moment that I came to the insight that has guided my counseling ever since. I realized that "Why is God doing this to me?" was not really a question about God. It was a cry of pain, and the person asking the question didn't need my theological wisdom. She needed a hug.

Ever since that day, my interactions with troubled or angry congregants have involved less explaining and more hand-holding. I have more than once paid a condolence call on a family to whom something so awful had happened that words seemed inadequate. So I didn't offer words, beyond "I'm sorry, I feel so bad for you." I would often sit quietly with the grieving widow or parent for several minutes, and when I would get up to go, the mourner would throw her arms around me and say, "Thank you for being here with us." My presence represented God's caring presence, the symbolic statement that God had not abandoned them. That reassurance, more than any theological wisdom, was what I was uniquely qualified to offer them.

Readers of my previous books will be familiar with the experience that changed my life and shaped my theology. When our son, our first child, was one year old, he stopped growing and stopped gaining weight. When he was three, his problem was diagnosed as progeria, the rapid-aging syndrome. He lived until the day after his fourteenth birthday, bravely, with a sense of humor and the capacity to inspire love in anyone who could look beyond appearances and get to know him.

Had I believed for an hour that God had chosen our son for this ordeal for whatever reason—to punish me for some long-forgotten offense, to inspire others with our example of fortitude—I would have left the rabbinate and never opened a prayer book or entered a synagogue again rather than pay homage to that God. Instead I was able to see God not as the source of our anguish but as the source of our ability to cope with it, to love and to comfort and to enjoy and ultimately to grieve for a very special child.

Had someone warned my wife and me on New Year's Day 1963, "Before this year is out, you will have a child with the following incurable problems. This is what it will mean for your marriage, for your family, for your ability to do your job. Can you handle that?" I am certain that I would have answered, "Please, we're only human. We know our limitations. That's too much to ask of us." But, as so often happens in life, Aaron came into our family without our permission having been asked, and from some source that I can only see as the spirit of God, we found the ability to give him what he needed, even as he, and God, gave us what we needed. "Only human" is a very misleading phrase. I have known and I have read about ordinary people who were able to do extraordinary things when they had to, in spite of their being "only human."

But whatever miracle God wrought for us, giving us the grace and strength to raise and love a child with a disfiguring, incurable disease, He worked an even greater miracle for Aaron. The miracle we prayed for was that modern medicine would come up with a cure for progeria. That did not happen. The miracle we got was a son who dealt bravely with an unfixable situation. We never saw him as a burden, as other families might have seen a child with severe medical issues. We felt blessed to have him as part of our family, and I give Aaron the credit for making that happen.

Rarely evincing self-pity, Aaron was bright, funny, feisty, kind, and brave. People who only knew him at a distance tended to react with pity. (The Afrikaans translation of *When Bad Things Happen to Good People* changed the title to *My Unfortunate Child*.) But people who knew him better saw his strengths more clearly than his limitations. Incredibly, more than a few envied him. After he died, a number of families named their own sons Aaron, to honor him and perhaps in the hope that their child would show some of the qualities that made Aaron so special.

Where does an afflicted seven- or ten- or twelve-year-old boy get all that courage and kindness from? I believe that was God doing for Aaron what He does for so many of His creatures in their hour of need.

Nor were we the exceptional case. God's gifts are available to people who are not conventionally religious. Our experience as parents of a child with serious health issues was more common than we might have imagined. Andrew Solomon wrote his best-selling book *Far from the Tree* (2012) as a study of children with autism, schizophrenia, deafness, and dwarfism, among other challenging conditions. He learned "how frequently parents who had supposed that they couldn't care for an exceptional child discover that they can." One mother of a child with Down syndrome told Solomon, "If I had had [amniocentesis], I would have terminated [the pregnancy], and I would have missed out on what has been not only the most difficult but also the most enriching experience of my life." As the Persian poet Rumi once wrote, "Light enters at the place of the wound."

Why do some youngsters flourish despite the bad

hand they are dealt by genetics, accidents, or being born into an unsupportive family, while others crash and burn, falling into bitterness and anger? That is a question I can't answer. I would never "blame the victim" by suggesting that God's help was available but they chose not to take advantage of it. All I can say is that miracles, by definition, don't happen all the time. That they happen at all is miracle enough.

I have come to find God in the quiet heroism of people who find themselves called on to do more than they ever believed they were capable of doing: the widow left alone without the companionship of family or the financial resources she needs, but who somehow manages to live a meaningful life; the parents of an autistic child who labor to raise their child, to love him, to find schools and employment for him, and the child himself, cast into a world that plays by rules he cannot always understand; the husband or wife caring for a spouse afflicted with Alzheimer's disease, loving him or her without any expectation of being loved in return; the commitment of men and women like Homer's lone fisherman, doing difficult jobs and earning less money in a year than many athletes and hedge fund managers earn in a week, because that is what life demands of them. I find God not in the tests that life imposes on us but in the always surprising capacity of ordinary men and women to rise to the occasion.

God does not send the problem; genetics, chance,

and bad luck do that. And God cannot make the problem go away, no matter how many prayers and good deeds we offer. What God does is promise us, I will be with you; you will feel burdened but you will never feel abandoned.

In July 2013, the Sterling and Francine Clark Art Institute in Williamstown, Massachusetts, put on a major exhibit of Winslow Homer's paintings, and the *New York Times* art critic Holland Cotter began his review of it by writing, "Winslow Homer was America's first great post-God landscape painter." What did he mean by calling the artist, one of whose works strikes me as proof of God, a "post-God landscape painter"? Before Homer, landscape art glorified nature as God's supreme handiwork. Cotter wrote, "In that art, Nature was a colossal, powerful moral consciousness; the human presence, if visible at all, an awe-struck speck." Those artists gave us paintings of soaring mountains, vast forests, towering waterfalls emptying into boundless lakes, dwarfing any human being in the picture. For Homer, by contrast, "people . . . are center stage. . . . Nature, the salvational force in earlier art, is now an enemy."

I find Cotter's analysis persuasive, but I differ with his use of the term "post-God." I, too, like those earlier artists, have found God's fingerprints, as it were, all over the natural world. I have lived in New England for almost fifty years, but my soul still thrills at the turning of the leaves every fall from green to stunning shades of red and orange. The back porch of our home, where I do a lot of my writing, offers a view of Lake Cochituate, the second-largest lake in Massachusetts, and on a sunny spring or summer day, I can be so mesmerized by the sight of sun on water that I can barely bring myself to write. I recognize God as the Author of Nature, but I don't see nature as "God made visible." Nature, as I have pointed out, can too often be harsh, unreliable, destructive. To me, the courage and determination of Homer's fisherman, not the terrifying storm that threatens him, speaks to the power and presence of God.

That insight, that God is to be found not in the crisis but in our response to the crisis, is the key to understanding one of the most important passages in the entire Bible. In chapter 3 of the book of Exodus, God speaks to Moses for the first time. Moses has fled Egypt after killing an Egyptian official who was beating an Israelite slave. God has taken note of that act of protest, and calls to Moses in a disembodied voice from a burning bush. He says, "I am the God of your father, the God of your ancestors. . . . I want you to go to Pharaoh and demand that he let the Israelites go" (Exodus 3:6, 10).

Moses responds, understandably, "Who am I that I should go to Pharaoh with that demand? Why should he listen to me?" (Exodus 3:11). God replies, *"Ehyeh imach,* I will be with you"* (verse 12). Moses then asks God, "When I go to the Israelites with that message [that God intends to set them free], and they ask me, In

whose name do you speak? what shall I say to them?"
(verse 13). God replies with a crucial answer that defies
easy translation and has provoked volumes of commentary: "My name is *Ehyeh asher ehyeh;* tell them that
Ehyeh sent you to them" (verse 14).

There are at least two puzzling things about that
exchange. The first is Moses's initial response. God
says to him, "I am the God of your forefathers. I want
you to go to Pharaoh and change the course of human
history," and Moses replies, "Who did you say was calling?" When Moses asks God, "What is Your name?" he
is not looking to clarify to whom he is speaking. In the
ancient world, one's name was more than just an identifying label. It declared something about who you were
and what you stood for. In Genesis 48:8, when Joseph
presents his sons Manasseh and Ephraim to his elderly
father, Jacob, Jacob asks him, "Who are they?" Jacob
knows their names; he has just been told that. But he is
meeting them for the first time and he wants to know,
given that they have an Israelite father and an Egyptian
mother, what sort of young people they are, what their
values are. Similarly, when Moses responds to God's
charge by asking, "What is Your name?" he is asking,
"What sort of God are You? What do You stand for?"

God's answer, the untranslatable phrase *Ehyeh asher
ehyeh,* is even more puzzling than Moses's question. It
has been rendered "I am who I am" or "I will be what
I will be." Several theologians, who assume that when

God speaks, He speaks theology, translate it to mean "I am pure being" (whatever that means).

To me, the best and most helpful interpretation is that of the eleventh-century French Jewish commentator Rashi (*R*abbi *Sh*lomo son of *I*saac), who connects "*Ehyeh*" to its occurrence a few lines earlier, in Exodus 3:12. Moses challenges God, "Who am I that I should go to Pharaoh with that demand? Why should he listen to me?" God says to him, "*Ehyeh imach*, I will be with you."

Rashi seems to have been the first to note the connection between Exodus 3:12 and Exodus 3:14. God's Name, God's essential identity, is "the One who will be with you" when you have to do something you're afraid will be too hard for you. That makes a lot of sense to me. God is saying to Moses, as He will have occasion to say to every one of us, "*Ehyeh imach*": I won't do it for you, I won't do it without you, but I won't leave you to do it alone. I will be with you when you summon up the courage to do it, and I will give you qualities of strength and soul that you didn't know you were capable of.

In recent years, I have been introduced to a useful theological concept known as "second naïveté." I first came across it through my classmate Rabbi Neil Gillman, who went on after ordination to become a significant theologian and a masterful professor of religion. Gillman found it in the writings of Paul Tillich, one of the foremost theologians of the twentieth century, and of James Fowler, professor of the psychology of religion, though it has its roots in the writings of the French philosopher Paul Ricœur.

For Fowler, the development of a mature understanding of religious faith comes in three stages. There is the initial stage of "simple naïveté." Children believe everything they are told: that God watches over them and knows everything they do, that Santa Claus lives at the North Pole and has a dossier on who has been naughty and who has been nice, that everything in the Bible happened exactly as described, and that their parents know everything and can do anything. Believing those things helps children feel secure in an often overwhelming world. Fowler sees these articles of simple faith as the foundational "myths" of a child's faith and of Western culture.

Then, inevitably, shortly before or during adolescence, children realize that none of those myths are true, or at least not literally true. There is no Santa Claus, their parents are fallible human beings, and a lot of the Bible could not have happened as described. This is the traumatic second stage, the "breaking of the myths." At this point, many young people abandon religion altogether. If the Red Sea did not really split, if Methuselah did not really live to the age of 969, then the Bible is not true, and if it's not true, why should they take it seriously? And as we have seen in a number of best-selling books in recent years, a lot of very bright people never get beyond that disillusionment.

But Fowler's great contribution here, drawing on the work of Tillich, is to propose a third stage that goes beyond the "breaking of the myths," beyond adolescent skepticism and disillusionment. He calls it "second naïveté," and Neil Gillman defines it in his 2013 book *Believing and Its Tensions* as "recaptur[ing] the primary naïveté we had about the myth . . . with the conscious awareness that even though it might not be literally true, it can still be valuable."

We can reject the literal notion of Hell along the lines of Dante's Inferno, an actual location where bad people are punished for their sins. We can dismiss that as naive. But, calling on "second naïveté," can we believe that there are some things a person might do during his lifetime, the memory of which will haunt him for the rest of his days and make it hard for him to feel good about the kind of person he is? Can we believe that there are some moments in our lives that we can look back on, opportunities we missed that never came our way again, and bear the consequences of having missed that opportunity for as long as we live? "What might have been" is a pretty good definition of Hell.

We can outgrow the concept of a God who lives in Heaven and grants or denies our prayers. But can we grow beyond that adolescent skepticism and affirm the reality of a Power that replenishes our strength, our courage when we are about to feel we have no more strength or courage to call on? Can a Jewish family gather at the Seder table for Passover in joy and celebration, with memories of parents or grandparents who left Europe before the Holocaust, crossed an ocean, and came to America, and find it meaningful to praise a God who freed them from contemporary bondage, even if they are skeptical about the veracity of the Ten Plagues and the splitting of the Red Sea? And even after we have discarded any childish notion of our parents as all-knowing and all-powerful, can we recognize them as limited but loving, dedicated to us despite our flaws and theirs?

The concept of "second naïveté" enables us to shed the husks of ancient beliefs while continuing to cherish the valuable kernels of truth at their core.

My personal experience, and the experience of so many congregants and public figures, testifies to the validity of Rashi's interpretation and the truth of that promise. The God who is with us in our struggles, the God who is with us in our grieving, the God who is with us when we reach inside ourselves to try to find the capacity for forgiveness, the God who answers our prayers not by giving us what we ask for but by helping us realize that we already have it, is a God I have often met in my own life and in the experiences of many of my congregants. That God is a God I can believe in.

CHAPTER FOUR

Forgiveness Is a Favor
You Do Yourself

Revenge—getting even with someone who has done us wrong—is everybody's favorite sin. It is clearly a sin, but something about it feels virtuous. Revenge feels justified because it comes to us clad in the garments of justice. Someone has done wrong and that person should be held accountable. Shakespeare's Shylock sees it as second nature to a human being: "If you prick us, do we not bleed? If you tickle us, do we not laugh? If you poison us, do we not die? *And if you wrong us, shall we not revenge?*" (*The Merchant of Venice,* act 3, scene 1; italics mine).

And yet, for anyone who takes the Bible seriously, it is clearly forbidden. The complete verse in which we are told to love our neighbors as ourselves, Leviticus 19:18, tells us, "You shall not take vengeance or bear a grudge against your neighbor but you shall love your neighbor as yourself." From the context, the message would seem to be: cut your neighbor some slack for doing mean and hurtful things, because he is "as yourself," a flawed human being given to moments of selfishness and thoughtlessness, even as you are.

One commentator takes the point even farther, suggesting that it is not a coincidence that the injunction against revenge is found in the same verse as the injunction to love your neighbor as you love yourself. Martin Buber cites a Hasidic parable: Imagine yourself peeling an apple. You are holding the apple in your left hand and the knife in your right. The knife slips and cuts into your left hand. It hurts; it is painful and bleeding. What do you do? Does the left hand grab the knife and stab the right hand to get even? Of course not. Both hands are part of the same person. You would only be hurting yourself a second time. That, says Buber, is why we should not retaliate when someone has treated us badly. If he broke a law by what he did to you, the law should handle it. But when it comes to a conflict between two individuals, in the eyes of God, all human beings are part of a single body, a single entity fashioned in the image of God. To deliberately harm another person for hurting you is to harm yourself a second time, for the other person is "as yourself."

The rabbis in the Talmud explain the difference between vengeance and bearing a grudge with the following example: Vengeance is telling your neighbor,

"No, you can't borrow my shovel, because when you borrowed my ax you broke it." Bearing a grudge is telling him, "All right, you can borrow my shovel, even though when you borrowed my ax you broke it."

The rule against vengeance is clear enough, even though in many people it prompts the response, "You mean I should just let him get away with it?"

But expanding the prohibition to bearing a grudge is a bit puzzling. If you believe, as I do, that the Hebrew Bible does not hold us accountable for thought crimes, that the Torah forbids acts but never forbids ideas, thoughts, or feelings (we are commanded to revere God and to obey God, but there is no commandment to believe in God), Leviticus 19:18 would seem to forbid a thought. I'll have more to say about that later.

Why are we told not to get even with someone who has hurt us? Because when we do so, or even when we try to do so, we run the risk of lowering ourselves to his level. If we consider him to be a despicable human being, why would we be eager to imitate him? Nursing the effort to get even with someone who has hurt us has been compared to swallowing poison in the hope that it makes someone else sick. Moreover, when we are consumed by thoughts of getting back at such a person, we give that person even more power over us than he deserves.

Some years ago, my sermon on Yom Kippur was on the theme of forgiveness. I suggested that just as we ask God to forgive us for what we might have done wrong in the past year, reminding God that we are only human and can't be perfect, so should we forgive the people who have hurt us or offended us. They, too, are only human.

The day after Yom Kippur, a member of the congregation came to my office, very upset with me because of the sermon. She told me how her husband had left her several years ago for a younger woman and how, as a result, she has had to work two jobs to pay the bills and put food on the table, and has had to explain to her children why they can't have the video games all their friends have. She concluded, "And you want me to forgive him for what he's done to us?"

I told her, "That's right. I want you to forgive him. Not to excuse him, not to say that what he did was acceptable. It sounds like it was a very selfish thing he did. But I want you to forgive him for your sake, not for his. Why are you giving him the power to define you as a victim? Why are you giving him the power to define you in terms of what you don't have, a husband and an adequate income, instead of what you do have, a warm and loving home and two beautiful children?

"Do you realize what you are doing?" I asked her. "For six years, you've been holding a hot coal in your hand, looking for an opportunity to throw it at him. And for six years, he's been living comfortably with his new wife in New Jersey and you've burned your hand. Think of it this way: If he is no longer living in your house, why are you letting him live rent-free in your head? He doesn't deserve that. He doesn't deserve the energy you waste on being angry at him. You can evict him any time you choose to. You can take away his power to push your buttons and make you feel sorry for yourself."

Because the thirst for getting even is so powerful and so universal, great books, and a lot of bad books, have been written about it. In some of them, the innocent victim is successful and feels vindicated. In *The Count of Monte Cristo,* for example, Edmond Dantès is framed by three "friends" and sentenced to life in France's most notorious prison, only to escape, acquire a fortune, and concoct elaborate schemes to destroy his betrayers, all of which he feels good about afterward. To anyone who is sure he would enjoy that feeling of retribution, I would remind you that Edmond Dantès is a fictional character. In real life, people rarely feel good about what they have done. All too often, even if the avenger succeeds and survives, he or she may feel morally compromised for having done something so similar to what the perpetrator did to him. It has been suggested that taking the power to punish out of the hands of the aggrieved party and giving it to the central authority was one of the great steps forward in civilizing human beings, giving us impartial justice in place of vengeance.

But perhaps the greatest story ever written about revenge and forgiveness is found in the Bible, in the last chapters of Genesis, the story of Joseph and his brothers. You may remember the story from your Sunday school days. The patriarch Jacob has twelve sons, ten of them by his wife Leah and by the servant women, and the two youngest, Joseph and Benjamin, by his wife Rachel, whom he loved deeply and whose death in childbirth he continues to mourn. The older brothers are jealous of Joseph for being the father's favorite, and Joseph stokes their resentment by telling them of a dream he had that they would one day bow down to him. One day, while the older brothers are away pasturing the sheep, Jacob sends Joseph to see how they are doing. The brothers see him coming and are carried away by resentment. They seize him, strip him of the special coat his father had given him, and throw him into a pit. They now face a dilemma: what to do next. If they pull him out of the pit and take him home, he will tell their father what they did. They contemplate murdering him but shrink from the horror of that. Instead, they sell him as a slave to a passing caravan, and Joseph ends up as a servant in the household of an important Egyptian officer. Through a series of fortuitous events that make up one of the longest and most beguiling narratives in the Bible (about a quarter of the book of Genesis is devoted to his story), Joseph rises to become an important adviser to the Pharaoh of Egypt and saves Egypt from famine, but all the while, he never forgets his home and the series of events that led him to where he finds himself—"For I was kidnapped from the land of the Hebrews" (Genesis 40:15).

The famine brings everyone outside of Egypt to the brink of starvation. People come from all over the Middle East to beg for food and are willing to pay any price for it. One day, the sons of Jacob (all except Joseph's full brother, Benjamin) appear before Joseph to buy grain. He recognizes them, but they have no clue that the powerful Egyptian official, a man with the authority to give them food or send them home to starve, is the brother they mistreated ten years earlier. They bow before him, even as he once dreamed they would, and he realizes that this is his chance to pay them back for their cruelty to him. He toys with them, accusing them of coming to spy on Egypt, and demands that they prove they have been telling him the truth by producing their youngest brother, Benjamin. Their father had been reluctant to let Benjamin travel to Egypt. Were any harm to befall him, Jacob would lose the last remaining link to his beloved Rachel. But the alternative is starvation, so they return home and prevail on Jacob to let Benjamin go back to Egypt with them.

Joseph then springs an elaborate trap on them, arresting Benjamin and re-creating the situation in which his brothers had abandoned him into slavery. He wants to see how they will behave this time. The brothers panic. To return home without Benjamin would cause their father unbearable grief. They bicker among themselves as to whose idea it was to sell Joseph to the caravan in the first place. This is the moment Joseph has been dreaming of for years, his Edmond Dantès moment to do to them what they had done to him. Instead, he does something that I suspect surprises even himself. He says to them, "I am your brother Joseph. Is our father still alive?"

Why does he do that? After all those years of thirsting for revenge, dreaming of hurting them as they had hurt him, he decides that is not what he really wants. The Bible never explains why. It leaves it up to us to make sense of its narratives. But I can think of three reasons why Joseph rejects the chance to get even.

First, it may simply be that, contemplating doing to his brothers what they did to him, he realizes how wrong, how sordid it would feel. If it was monstrously evil when they did it, wouldn't it be equally evil for him to do it to them? To be sure, he has his reasons for wanting to hurt them. But ten years before, they had their reasons for resenting him and wanting to hurt him. He decides that he doesn't want to become like them and take pleasure in hurting another person, just because he can.

Second, finding himself in a position in which he has to choose between avenging what was done to him and having a family, he chooses family. Remember, for ten years Joseph has been the only Israelite in all of

Egypt. He has power and prestige, but he is constantly reminded that he is a foreigner. To perpetuate the bitterness between brothers rather than heal the breach would leave him permanently alone. He chooses to forgive his brothers for what they did years before so that he, like everyone around him, can have a family.

When I was growing up in Brooklyn in the 1940s and '50s, I heard many stories about my extended family and many families we were friendly with, of relatives with whom other relatives were not on speaking terms. The reasons went back many years, often more than a generation. Somebody refused to lend someone money, or else borrowed money and didn't repay it. Somebody wasn't invited to a daughter's wedding, or was invited and chose not to attend. Often, the reason had long been forgotten; children were simply told, "We don't speak to Uncle So-and-so's grandchildren." As a result, siblings went years without speaking to one another, until thrown together at a funeral, and sometimes not even then. I can recall instances, at funerals at which I officiated, of being asked to give two or three locations for the memorial week of shivah, because the several adult children of the deceased were not on speaking terms. And it always struck me as so sad and so unnecessary. Joseph in the Bible may have felt the same way.

But the third reason, as I understand the story, is the most important and is the essential point I want to make. The thirst for revenge is not about justice, it is about power. Someone has hurt you, someone has cheated you, and you feel powerless to do anything about it. He has exercised power over you and you yearn to reclaim that power, to be able to hurt him as he hurt you. You are so frustrated by that sense of powerlessness that you never recognize that you are the one who perpetuates it by insisting on holding on to the memory. The woman who challenged me about my Yom Kippur sermon, telling me how hard her life had been since her husband left her, needed to understand that the only power she still had over her ex-husband was the power to expel him from her mind, to take away his ability to define her as an undesirable, unlovable victim. She didn't have the power to solve her financial problems herself, and there was no undoing what he had done to her and the children, but she and no one else had the power to stop dwelling on it, because it was her dwelling that perpetuated her feelings of victimhood.

I tried to make this point to the young woman who came up to me after a speech I had given and told me how, five years earlier, she had lost out on a fellowship because the woman who prevailed over her had been having an affair with the professor who chose the recipient. She tried to file a complaint against him but was told that it would be a "he said, she said" situation, that he would accuse her of being vindictive because she didn't win the prize, and that it probably would not do her any good in the short or long run. She asked me what she should do about it, and I told her it sounded like there wasn't a whole lot she could do except chalk it up to life's unfairness. "You mean I should let him get away with it?" she said. I pointed out to her that he had already gotten away with it. She had no power to rewrite history. The only power she had was the power to stop obsessing about it and evict the incident from her thoughts. "Until you do that," I told her, "you are perpetuating your role as victim. Keep doing that long enough and you may not be able to see yourself in any other role. You don't want that. You and you alone have the power to free yourself from that role.

"Yes, it's unfair," I told her, "and I'm sorry it happened. But think of it this way: the two people who cheated you of something you deserved sold out their integrity for a few hours of sexual pleasure and a two-year fellowship that has already ended. That's a bad bargain. Any time you give away your integrity, whether it's to consummate an affair or win an election, you lose more than you gain. You have to live the rest of your life with the knowledge that you are a cheater. You kept your integrity, and in the long run, that will serve you well. Wash that man out of your hair and go forward to have the life you deserve."

That way of looking at things will resolve the puzzle I set forth at the beginning of this chapter. If the Bible holds us accountable for our deeds but not for our thoughts or beliefs, why is it a sin, according to

Leviticus 19, to bear a grudge if we don't act on it? I see nurturing a grudge as another way in which we let the offending party continue to wield power over us. If we can't forget the incident and go on with our lives, the offender continues to live in our heads, making us feel powerless. He's not entitled to that power, so why should we give it to him?

Seeing forgiveness as an active deed rather than a passive one, seeing the thirst for revenge as an unseemly wish and letting go of it as a matter of reclaiming power, gives me the answer to the most challenging question I am ever asked when I speak on this topic: "Are you saying that we should forgive the Nazis for the Holocaust?" My answer is, "If by forgiveness, you mean excusing them, saying something along the lines of 'Things happen in war, people get carried away, let's put it behind us because my religion tells me to forgive anyone who has hurt me,' then I would say no, absolutely not. I'm not prepared to say that. I want everyone who was a part of the Holocaust to be held accountable for what he did. I want to track down every last ninety-year-old Nazi former concentration camp guard who is still alive and bring him to trial for crimes against humanity. I want to track down all the works of art looted from Jewish owners and, if we can't find descendants of the original owners, give them to a Jewish museum. I want those things not because I am a vindictive person but because I pay those elderly war criminals the compliment of seeing them as human beings, and human beings are responsible for what they do."

But when I speak of forgiveness in the context of the Holocaust, what I am saying is that I don't want the searing memory of the Holocaust to take over my mind, infecting everything I think or do. I don't want to think of Judaism as a synonym for victimhood. I don't want the memory of the Holocaust to make me suspect that anyone who criticizes Israel is a crypto-Nazi. Hitler has been dead for seventy years. He doesn't deserve the power to infect my mind and make me suspect all gentiles of being secret Nazis. What I want the memory of the Holocaust, and the slogan "Never again," to do is the precise opposite of that. I want it to immunize me against the danger of any effort to stigmatize an entire group of people—be it gays, Muslims, or political conservatives—as being a mortal danger to our way of life. I will criticize individuals when they deserve criticism, but I will not condemn entire populations. We have seen where that leads.

There is one other dimension to the issue of forgiveness. It's a lot easier to forgive when the one who has offended us recognizes the wrongness of what he did or said and utters the magic words "I'm sorry." Think of how we react to the politician who takes responsibility for something that went wrong, who says, "I'm sorry. I should have responded sooner. I should have known what people in my office were doing. I hope I've learned my lesson from this and will do better next time." Compare that to the public figure who responds, "Mistakes were made, and I intend to find out who let me down by doing that."

There is a story in the Bible about two people who loved each other very much. Because they loved each other so much, they had the power to hurt each other with a careless word or deed, and one time, when they did, they were too hurt and too proud to say "I'm sorry." The story is found in the second book of Samuel, chapter 6, verses 12 to 23, and the last verse of the story is, in my opinion, the saddest verse in the entire Bible.

King Saul and all of his sons have died in battle against the Philistines. The immensely popular David is chosen to be king over both the northern and southern Israelite tribal federations. In an effort to unify the country, David conquers the Jebusite citadel of Jerusalem situated on the border between northern and southern Israel, and he establishes it as his capital. (Washington, D.C., was chosen as the capital of the United States on a similar basis.)

Then, to make Jerusalem the religious as well as political center of Israel, he arranges to bring the Ark of the Covenant, housing the original tablets of the Ten Commandments, to that city in a festive procession marked by singing, dancing, and celebrating. We read (2 Samuel 6:14), "David danced with all his might before the Lord, while wearing a linen ephod" (a kind of

robe). David's wife Michal, daughter of the former king
Saul, was watching the celebration from her window.
We are not told why she was not among the celebrants,
whether she was uncomfortable in crowds or just found
it beneath her dignity. But when the celebration ended
and David came home flushed with triumph, his wife
greeted him by saying sarcastically, "Didn't the king of
Israel do himself honor today, exposing himself in the
sight of the servant women, the way a worthless person
might do?" Why does she say that? Perhaps she feels
left out of all the celebrating. Perhaps, remembering
her father, she has a different idea of how a king should
behave. In effect, she is saying to David, "I didn't grow
up on a sheep farm the way you did. I grew up in a
palace, and I know how a king should behave, with a
measure of dignity."

David is deeply wounded by his wife's words. Not
only has she spoiled the greatest day of his life, she has
reminded him that he did not become king by the normal process of succession. He became king after the
previous king and all his sons were killed in a war that
David chose to avoid. Hurt and angry, he responds to
Michal, "I wasn't dancing before servant girls. I was
dancing before the Lord." But because he is hurt and
angry, he cannot stop there. Michal has hurt him and he
feels the need to hurt her back. He goes on to say, "I was
dancing before the Lord, *who rejected your father and your
whole family and made me king in their place*" (2 Sam-

uel 6:21; italics mine). And then we read what I think is the saddest verse in the Bible: "And Michal daughter of Saul never had a child to the day she died" (6:23).

I take that to mean that David and Michal never approached each other intimately as husband and wife after that argument, and I find that so sad. Theirs was one of the great love stories in the Bible. Michal is the only woman in Scripture described as falling in love with a man. Twice she defied her father the king to protect David. David repeatedly risked his life to win her after King Saul set a dowry of one hundred dead Philistines for her hand. But one argument and the stubborn refusal to apologize and say "I'm sorry," on both of their parts, destroyed all that love. David would spend the rest of his life collecting wives, sometimes other men's wives, in what I understand to be a quest to recapture what he once had with Michal. She, for her part, would live out her days haunting the corridors of the palace, pitied by all who saw her as the "unwanted wife." And all it would have taken was for one of them to say, "I'm sorry," and for the other to accept the apology, to forgive, and to say, "I'm sorry, too."

If the 1970 movie *Love Story* is remembered at all some forty-five years after it came out, it will be remembered for two things. One is the phenomenon of tens of thousands of American women in their forties named Jennifer, after the heroine of the movie. The other is what may be the dumbest advertising slogan ever devised for a major motion picture. If you were of moviegoing age back then, you may remember it: "Love means never having to say you're sorry." Maybe the publicists for the movie were trying to say that if two people truly love each other, they will forgive each other for any slight or offense, without an apology being needed. But, as the story of David and Michal would warn us, and as the experience of most people reading this chapter will confirm, it is possible to be deeply wounded by an act of thoughtlessness on the part of someone you love. That may be even more wounding than having something done to you by a casual acquaintance. But a simple apology, saying "I'm sorry," may be all it takes to salve the wound.

Nelson Mandela led the black majority population of South Africa from being severely discriminated against to being the rulers of their country. Mandela realized that he personally and his people could never be free without forgiving their oppressors. When Mandela was confined to prison on Robben Island, his body was in prison. Had he continued to hate the Afrikaner minority that was repressing his people (and they had richly earned his hatred), his mind and his soul would have been imprisoned as well, imprisoned by feelings of bitterness and impotence and a desire for revenge that he was in no position to carry out. Once he exercised his power to banish hatred and thoughts of vengeance from his mind, he felt free enough (and strong enough) to work for his people's freedom.

Those who fought for civil rights in the American south in the 1960s and '70s largely employed a similar tactic. Led by Martin Luther King Jr., they tried to cleanse their minds of hatred so that the righteousness of their cause would not be compromised. Rather than fight fire with fire against an enemy who had more firepower than they did, they fought fire with water, letting the righteousness of their cause prevail over the forces of hatred.

When I was a boy in the 1930s and '40s, my parents had friends who had earned PhD degrees and were qualified to be college professors, but they ended up teaching in high schools because universities would not hire Jews. Ben Eisenstadt graduated from law school with honors, but no law firm would hire him. He went on to come up with a method of putting single servings of sugar in little packets, and then to invent Sweet'N Low, becoming wealthier than many lawyers in the process. For the most part, Jews who faced social and professional discrimination during and after the Depression did not take advantage of their later success by discriminating against other vulnerable populations. Instead, they were disproportionately active in virtually every civil rights and minority rights effort. They used their newfound power not to get even, not to pull up the ladder they had climbed to make sure that no one could climb it after them, but by remembering what it felt like to be discriminated against and refusing to do that to other human beings who were, after all, "like themselves."

This is the knowledge I would share with you: nursing a grudge only perpetuates the offender's power over you. He continues to live in your head, reinforcing your frustration, polluting your imagination with thoughts of getting even. Don't let him get away with that. He may or may not deserve forgiveness, but you deserve better than to waste your energy being angry at him. Letting go is the best revenge. Forgiveness is the identifying marker of the stronger party to the dispute. It is truly a favor you do yourself, not an undeserved gesture to the person who hurt you. Be kind to yourself and forgive.

CHAPTER FIVE

Some Things Are Just Wrong; Knowing That Makes Us Human

What is the most important difference between human beings and other living creatures? A larger brain? Upright posture? The power of speech? I would maintain that it is the possession of a conscience, the innate awareness that some things are wrong and should not be done. Animals can understand that some actions are dangerous. Domesticated animals and household pets learn that certain behaviors will lead to their being punished. Animals can be useful and loyal, but they cannot be good, because goodness involves making moral calculations, sensing the rightness or wrongness of some actions, not only of their consequences. "Good doggie" is no more a moral statement than "good weather." Human beings are the only creatures blessed, or burdened, with a conscience, the awareness that there are some things we simply should not do.

There is a story in the Bible that makes this point, that knowing the difference between good and bad is what raises human beings above the animal level. It is found in chapter 22 of the book of Numbers, and it may be the only funny story in the Bible. It is the story of the wizard Balaam and his talking donkey.

The king of the Moabites is alarmed by the movement of the Israelite throng through the desert toward his kingdom. Dimly aware that the Israelites are operating under divine guidance, he hires the renowned wizard and caster of spells Balaam to curse the Israelites so that they will represent no threat to his kingdom. (If Balaam is such an accomplished wizard, "for I know whomever you bless is blessed and whomever you curse is cursed" [Numbers 22:6], why doesn't the king hire him to bless his own nation? Because for some people, hatred of the "other" is a more powerful force than love for your own kin.) Balaam is reluctant to take on the assignment, but the king offers him a lot of money and he agrees.

Balaam sets out in the direction of the Israelite camp, riding his donkey. God intervenes to stop him by sending an angel to block his path. The donkey sees the angel and intuits that what they are doing is going against the will of God, but Balaam, his eyes blinded by the prospect of a major payday, cannot see it. He strikes the donkey to get it moving again. This happens a second and then a third time. After the third time, an exasperated Balaam whips the donkey, at which point "God opens the donkey's mouth" and it says to its owner, "Why are you hitting me? Am I not your faithful donkey?" (Numbers 22:28). God then opens Balaam's eyes and he sees the angel of the Lord blocking his path. He understands that what he is doing is against the will of God. God will put words in his mouth blessing Israel instead of cursing them.

What is going on here? Any time you have a story in which animals speak, whether it is a biblical parable or a Walt Disney cartoon, it raises the question of what makes humans different from animals. In the story of Balaam, the point is that human beings should know the difference between right and wrong. If an animal can see the wrongness of something and a person is blind to it, the person's humanity is deficient. Greed and fear can drive a person to forfeit his humanity and become even less than a beast, as happened to Balaam.

This sense of the wrongness of some things is not learned as we grow up, like arithmetic. It is innate. In the spring of 2013, I was invited to speak to my grandson's science class at Tufts University on the relationship between science and religion, between truth and faith. The class took place only a few days after terrorists had set off bombs near the finish line of the Boston Marathon, just a few miles from the university, killing several people and injuring hundreds more. Boston was still reeling from the tragedy. I challenged the students, "Tell me why setting off a bomb in a crowd was wrong, not just against the law, not just a matter of taste, but absolutely wrong, on a purely rational basis, without appealing to your emotional response." They couldn't do it. There are laws against murder, but something like the Boston Marathon bombing elicits a different reaction than other violations. We not only feel it is illegal; it violates our notion of what it means to be a human being. We feel it is Wrong with a capital *W*.

The definitions of what those things are may have changed at the margins over the centuries as our understanding of those to whom we owe sympathy has expanded from family to community to nation, and finally to all humanity. The definition of acceptable or unacceptable behavior may vary slightly from one society to another, but a basic awareness of good and bad behavior seems universal.

Even very young children seem to understand that. They know how to protest "That's not fair" if a parent or nursery school teacher does something that violates their innate sense of fairness. In his 2013 book *Just Babies: The Origins of Good and Evil*, the psychologist Paul Bloom shares studies indicating that even very young children seem to have an innate negative response to unfairness and to the uneven application of reward and punishment.

In one experiment cited by Bloom, one-year-olds were shown a puppet show featuring a good puppet who returned a ball to its owner and a selfish puppet who kept the ball for himself. The puppets were then each given a treat, and the children were told that they could take the treat away from either puppet or both puppets if they wanted to. Just about all the children took the treat away from the selfish puppet. Studies have shown that even virtual newborns are distressed by the sound of another baby crying and show a desire to comfort the crying infant.

Bloom concludes that "developmental psychology, supported by evolutionary biology and cultural anthropology, favors the view . . . that some aspects of morality come naturally to us." These would include a moral sense, the ability to know the difference between kind and cruel actions; a sense of fairness, the need to treat others equally and appropriately; a sense of empathy and compassion, feeling pain at the suffering of others; and a rudimentary sense of justice, the desire to see good actions rewarded and bad actions punished. In Bloom's view, these moral foundations do not have to be taught. They are "the products of biological evolution." Bloom concludes, "Babies are moral animals, equipped by evolution with empathy and compassion, the capacity to judge the actions of others, and even some rudimentary understanding of justice and fairness." No other living creature can be described that way.

What we do need to be taught are the boundaries defining to whom we owe that empathy. That is something we have learned slowly over the generations, so that things once considered acceptable when done to people to whom we owed no loyalty or with whom we shared no sense of kinship—torture, slavery, the mistreatment of females, discrimination against people of other races or nations—are no longer acceptable in most quarters.

There are some people who are psychopaths, who seem to lack that sense of empathy entirely. They have no hesitation, no discomfort with being cruel to others. Fortunately, such people are rare, perhaps 1 percent of the population. There are others who feel so hurt and angry by someone else's mistreatment of them that they will try to reclaim their sense of importance by exercising power over someone else—a wife, a child, a vulnerable stranger. But then there are the rest of us. Adam Smith, writing 250 years ago in his book *The Theory of Moral Sentiments,* theorized that the human being was defined by his or her ability to see another person in pain and "place ourselves in his situation . . . to become in some measure the same person with him and even feel" what the other person was feeling. In our own time, scientists have confirmed that ability. As Bloom has written in "The Baby in the Well: The Case Against Empathy," an article he published in *The New Yorker* in May 2013, it seems that "some of the same neural systems that are active when we are in pain become engaged when we observe the suffering of others."

Where does this conviction of the wrongness of some behavior come from? As I've said, the source cannot be as simple as rational thought; the benefits of lying and stealing can make those things seem objectively attractive, and we know that there are people who resort to them even as they know they are wrong.

Some people find the fingerprints of God all over our innate sense of justice and compassion, our ability to feel the pain of a stranger whom we do not know and with whom we have little in common other than shared humanity. In *Just Babies,* Bloom speaks of how the religious thinker C. S. Lewis characterizes our ability to care about people who have no connection to us as "the voice of God within our souls." And he mentions, too, the eminent scientist Dr. Francis Collins, director of the National Institutes of Health for the federal government and a deeply religious man, who puts it even more strongly. At some point in human evolution, Dr. Collins believes, "God literally restructured the human brain" so that we developed the capacity for altruism and empathy, so that we learned to recognize the rightness of some things (giving blood, rushing to aid the victim of an accident) and the wrongness of others (slavery, child abuse). These things are not logical conclusions.

In 2013, the best-selling author Elizabeth Gilbert wrote a novel, *The Signature of All Things,* whose heroine, Alma Whittaker, independently comes up with a theory of evolution through natural selection very much like that of her contemporary Charles Darwin. Her last unanswered question concerns the evolutionary value of altruism. Traits that make a person's survival more likely have obvious evolutionary value and make for a greater likelihood of that person passing on his or her genes to a child. But what about people who risk their lives for the sake of others, "the men who rushed into fires to rescue strangers, and the starving prisoners who shared their last bites of food with other starving prisoners"? There is no survival advantage there.

In an imagined conversation, Whittaker puts the question to Alfred Russel Wallace, a contemporary and colleague of Darwin's who shared his faith in natural selection. His answer (and remember, this is a fictional account but based on extensive research): "We have [these altruistic impulses] because there is a supreme intelligence in the universe, which wishes for communion with us. This supreme intelligence longs to be known. It calls out to us . . . and grants us these remarkable minds, in order that we try to reach for it." In other words, the evolutionary advantage conferred by the impulse to altruism is not that it helps us live longer but that it helps us live more deeply. It confers on us the profound experience of being touched by God.

Two personal stories: I have a friend, a sports re-
porter for a Boston television station, with whom I get
together once a month for coffee and a chance to talk
about the local sports teams. We started meeting shortly
after he moved to the Boston area and realized that the
author of *When Bad Things Happen to Good People* lived
in the town next to his. He thought I would appreciate
his story.

Not long before we met, he had volunteered to be
a bone marrow donor for a total stranger for whom he
was a match. It was a complicated process, uncomfortable, and with a slight risk to his health, but he chose to
do it. He couldn't explain why except that it felt right. He
had the ability to save someone's life and he could not
say no to that. I appreciated his story and the short book
he wrote about it, and we have been friends ever since.

A second story: My wife and I support some two
dozen or more charitable causes. Some are health-related,
some are religious, and some do good things in our
town. A few years ago, my wife called my attention to a
habit I had developed. When I am working on a book, an
article, or a sermon, I write in the morning for an hour
or two. Before I sit down to write, I make out a check
to one of the charitable causes we support. At first, I
insisted it was just a matter of cleaning an envelope off
my desk so that I would have room to write. But my wife
persuaded me that there was more to it than that. I was
preparing myself for the challenge of being creative by

doing an act of kindness and generosity, thereby defining myself as a certain kind of person, and that perspective would flavor my writing.

Where does the impulse to altruism come from? Where does our instinctive horror at accounts of cruelty come from? There is a story in the Bible about how human beings acquired a conscience. You have all heard it many times, you have all read it, but you probably didn't realize that that was what it was about, because its meaning has been distorted for almost two thousand years. It is the story of Adam and Eve in the Garden of Eden, and we find it in chapter 3 of Genesis.

We have all grown up with the idea that Genesis 3 is the story of the Fall, the account of Original Sin, defining human beings as disobedient sinners. Adam and Eve were tested by being given one rule by God: Don't eat from that particular tree. They broke that rule, and human beings have been estranged from God ever since and need to seek reconciliation. Thus John Milton begins his epic poem *Paradise Lost* with the words:

> *Of Man's first disobedience, and the fruit*
> *Of that forbidden tree whose mortal taste*
> *Brought death into the World, and all our woe,*
> *With loss of Eden . . .*

The clear implication is that if Adam and Eve had not disobeyed God by violating His one rule, they could have lived forever in Paradise. The problem is, I don't think that is what the third chapter of Genesis was originally meant to teach us.

The text of Genesis 3 was probably written down around 1000 BCE and was based on much older material well known at the time. But our understanding of the story has been shaped by interpreters, both Christian and Jewish, who lived many hundreds of years later. Not only were they as removed from the time of the original version of the story as we are from the time of Charlemagne, they lived in a very different cultural world than did the people who first told the story.

In the early centuries of the Common Era, the time of the origin of Christianity and of the compilation of the Talmud that defined Judaism after the destruction of the Jerusalem Temple, the land of Judea was part of the Roman Empire and its culture was dominated by what is known as Hellenism, Greek culture blended with Roman imperial power. The scholar Tikva Frymer-Kensky has summarized a crucial dimension of Hellenism in her 1989 article "The Ideology of Gender in the Bible and the Ancient Near East." She writes: "The Greek philosophical system viewed the male-female polarity as the major axis of their thinking. . . . Men embodied all those characteristics that the Greeks considered the highest achievements of their civilization, and woman, by contrast, had all the characteristics that the Greeks denigrated and discarded." Men achieved great things while women were no more than decorations or distractions.

Think back to Homer's *Iliad*, which predated Hellenism but continued to influence Greek thought. True love is found between male warriors; women are trophies to be used and discarded. Aristotle seems to have believed that a man's sperm created a baby, which he then deposited in a woman's womb to grow, freeing him up to do nobler things. No wonder, then, that Genesis 3 was misunderstood as a parable of how female weakness brought sin and death into the world, creating in corners of Judaism and Christianity alike the notion that women should be modestly dressed, if not kept completely out of sight, lest they tempt men into misbehavior, as Eve did to Adam.

What would a plausible reading of Genesis 3 look like if it were drawn from the biblical text without the overlay of two thousand years of misogynistic misunderstanding? We begin with Eve being fashioned out of Adam's rib, as an afterthought of Creation. In all of our current and medieval Bible translations, the Hebrew word "*tzela*" is rendered "rib." It can mean "rib," but it can also mean "side," and it appears more often in that sense in Scripture, especially in the Exodus narratives of the construction of the Tabernacle. Two highly respected Jewish commentators, Rabbi Samuel ben Nachman in the third century and Rashi, the preeminent commentator on the Torah, in the eleventh, both take the word to mean "side," as do several early Christian translations.

That meaning would give us a Genesis narrative in which "God created Man in His image, *male and female He created them*" (Genesis 1:27; italics mine). The first human was a double person, like a set of conjoined twins, with a male side and a female side. In Plato's *Symposium,* Aristophanes gives his theory of the origin of love. When the gods created the first human beings, each one was a double person, with a male side and a female side. These double creatures were so powerful that the gods felt threatened by them. So they cut each in half, and ever since then, everyone has gone through life looking for the partner who will make him or her complete. (A similar fable is found in the Talmud.)

Doesn't that sound a lot like the Genesis account of how God could not find a proper mate for this hybrid human? So "the Lord God cast a deep sleep on the Man, and while he slept, God separated one of his sides [not 'ribs'], closed the flesh at the site of the division, fashioned it into a woman, and brought her to the man. . . . Hence a man leaves his father and mother and cleaves unto his wife, *and they become one flesh*" (Genesis 2:21–22, 24; italics mine). That is, animals are drawn by instinct to mate and reproduce. When our family dog came into heat, we mated her with a male dog whom she had never seen before and would never see again, and she gave birth to five puppies. But for humans, blessed and burdened with a conscience, mating can never be that impersonal. It matters to us whom we share our bodies with. We seek not only sexual pleasure but a sense of wholeness, to become "one flesh." Our notion of self expands to include another person and eventually to include children. Human beings seem to be the only living creatures who join in sexual union face-to-face, because only for humans does it matter whom you are coupling with.

So if the rib is not a rib, is the fruit still a forbidden fruit? I find it instructive that when God confronts Adam and Eve after they have eaten of the Tree of Knowledge of Good and Bad, God never uses the word "sin" or "punishment." God never calls what they did a sin. There is no reference to the event or to the notion of Original Sin resulting from it in any of the Hebrew prophets, who frequently chastise Israel for all manner of misbehavior. They never accuse Israel of being like their disobedient original ancestors. As I read it, what God spells out for Adam and Eve in the wake of their eating the fruit is not "punishment" but "consequence," and the key to understanding it is remembering the name of the fruit. It was not "the fruit you're not supposed to eat." It was "the fruit of the Tree of Knowledge of Good and Bad." Eating it ushers them into a world that animals will never know. Sexual activity, which comes so naturally, so free of complications for other creatures, will be a source of complexity and concern for humans, a powerful urge surrounded by rules of right and wrong ways to exercise it. For many of us, it will be the most morally and emotionally complicated thing we will engage in.

Animals give birth to their young with a minimum of discomfort and spend a minimal amount of time rearing their young before sending them on their way. For human females, giving birth may be the most physically painful experience they will ever undergo. But the physical pain of giving birth is not the essential result of eating the fruit of the Tree of Knowledge of Good and Bad. The standard translation of God's words to Eve after she has eaten the fruit is "In pain shall you bear children" (Genesis 3:16). But the word translated "pain" is not the usual Hebrew word for physical pain. The word is "*etzev,*" and it means something like "anguish" or "sorrow." Interestingly, it occurs again in Genesis 6:6. Contemplating the widespread human misbehavior in the time of Noah, we read that "God regretted having made human beings on the earth, and He *grieved* in His heart" (italics mine).

Might it be that God, speaking to Adam and Eve in Genesis 3, is not so much punishing Eve for gaining a knowledge of Good and Bad as alerting her to the anguish it will cause her? She will know that some things are wrong; she will see her children doing them and will be powerless to stop them. I suspect many parents will agree that the real pain of having children is not the physical pain of giving birth to them but the anguish of seeing your child choose a path in life of which you do not approve.

In a similar way, God's words to Adam, "By the sweat of your brow will you earn bread to eat" (Genesis 3:19), can be seen as anticipating the difference between animals, who instinctively know how to find food, and humans, who have to prepare themselves for careers and worry about finding, and then keeping, a job.

And yet, I suspect most of us would testify that parenthood and creativity at work are among the most rewarding, if also the most challenging, dimensions of our lives. They are the things that make us human.

The first thing that happens to Adam and Eve after they gain a knowledge of Good and Bad—that is, after they develop a conscience—is that they realize they are naked and are embarrassed (Genesis 3:7). We read that and we think to ourselves, Well, of course. Anyone would be embarrassed to be outdoors with no clothes on. But I would remind you that they are literally the only people in the world. There is no one to see them. I understand their embarrassment as resulting not from their nudity but from the new awareness, born of eating the fruit of the Tree of Knowledge of Good and Bad, that they are subject to being scrutinized and evaluated as moral actors. They now understand that there are right things that should be done and wrong things that should not be done, and that there is a power in the world entitled to judge them.

Eve, in my understanding of the story, is not the villain whose vulnerability to temptation brought misery into the world. That is a distortion born of misogynist, Hellenistic bias, and perhaps a need to put women down. She is the heroine. If having a conscience, knowing the difference between Good and Bad, is what makes humans different from other creatures, Eve is the first human being, bravely stepping across the line that separates humans from other creatures and inviting her husband to follow her.

Adam and Eve's feeling self-conscious about their nakedness tells me that what they are feeling after having broken God's rule is not guilt but shame, the sense of being judged. Erik Erikson, in his masterful book *Childhood and Society* (1959), distinguishes between shame and guilt. Shame is external and visual. It involves being seen and judged by an outside authority. For Erikson, "shame supposes that one is completely exposed and conscious of being looked at—in a word, self-conscious." Darwin once wrote that human beings are the only animals that blush, to which Mark Twain added the comment, "Or need to." Guilt, by contrast, is internal, the sense of a voice inside our heads passing judgment on what we have done. What Adam and Eve are described as feeling is shame, the sense of being seen and judged.

If this reading of Genesis 3 is correct, cleansed of antifeminine Hellenistic prejudice, the biblical teaching would be that what we inherited from our first ancestors was not Original Sin but Original Virtue, the uniquely human gift and burden of being able to know right from wrong, good from bad.

Needless to say, I don't take the story of the expulsion from Eden literally. I don't think humans acquired a conscience as the result of an encounter with a talking snake. I take it as a metaphor for the remarkable evolutionary emergence of a unique creature, one who shared with the other animals the basic needs to eat, sleep, and mate but had the unique capacity to override instinct and refrain from doing things they understood to be wrong.

Woodstock, the 1969 music festival, came at a time when our country was split over the war in Vietnam. It was billed as "three days of peace and music." (The quip at the time was: "If you can remember it, you probably weren't there.") It grew beyond the planners' expectations, with an estimated four hundred thousand young people enduring steady rain and mud to see the performers and hear the music that defined the counter-cultural generation. As much as any single event, it put a spotlight on the gap between young people, who saw it as an expression of what life could be like cleansed of society's hypocritical hang-ups, and their parents' generation, who were repelled by what they saw as an orgy of loud music, drugs, and casual sex.

In 1969, I was caught between the generations. I was in my midthirties, too old (and too religious and too settled with a wife and family) to be part of the Woodstock generation, but young enough to appreciate what they claimed to stand for. They were rebelling against what they saw as the selfishness and shallowness of the things their parents celebrated. But I was put off by what they sought to replace it with. I see Yasgur's farm, where the festival was taking place, as representing to them the purity of the Garden of Eden before Eve ate the apple, a world where there were no rules limiting one's access to drugs, drink, or casual sex. It would be the life of a free spirit unrestrained by society's rules, uncontaminated by a sense of Sin. The documentary movie *Woodstock* seemed to capture that sense of Eden before the Fall, with eating, drinking, and using drugs without restriction, casual nudity, and sex between people who didn't know each other's names. To festivalgoers, that must have felt like Paradise. To me, it represented a regression to living like animals, shedding all sense of permitted and forbidden, eating and mating without reflection, as if Eve had never tasted the fruit of the Tree of Knowledge of Good and Bad.

I admire the idealism of young people, their determination not to replicate the hypocrisies and narrowly focused lives of their parents. I am also aware that Woodstock took place almost half a century ago and there was a war going on in Vietnam that many people saw as unjustified, a war that divided the country and exposed these young people to the draft, asking them to risk their lives for a cause they weren't sure they believed in (unlike their parents' war, World War II). Those young people who yearned to get their souls free are now middle-aged and possibly grandparents. I wonder how they feel about that summer now. The lesson of Genesis 3, as I have come to understand it, is that our souls don't really yearn to be free. Our souls yearn to be guided, to be focused on what makes us human. Yes, from time to time we are tempted to throw off the restraints of civilization (think of the way Mardi Gras is celebrated on the eve of Lent in some cultures). But we realize soon enough that the freedom of living like an animal—no clothes, no schedules, no rules to adhere to, and the ability to mate with any available partner—grows stale. True fulfillment comes in living as Adam and Eve did *after* they left the Garden, finding wholeness with each other, finding work that dignified them with the feeling of competence, and raising a family.

I am grateful to Adam and Eve (who, I would remind you, are not historical figures but symbolic representatives of the emergence of a marvelous new creature on our planet) for bequeathing to us a sense of Sin. I am not proud of the wrong things I have done over the course of my eighty years of life, the white lies I have told, and the opportunities to do good that I have spurned. I don't think I'm a terrible person; in fact, I think I'm a pretty good person. And one of the things that makes me a good person is the religion-based awareness that I could and should be better. Without the knowledge that some things are wrong, I would lack that knowledge of Good and Bad that was the gift to humanity of the "forbidden fruit" and is the trait that defines us as human.

Which leads me to another problem I have with the traditional understanding of the Garden of Eden story, the one that sees it as an act of disobedience toward God's laws, passing on the inherited stain of Original Sin to all of Adam and Eve's descendants. I'm not comfortable criticizing another person's theology, but, try as I may, I don't find the notion of inherited guilt anywhere in the Bible.

There is a verse in Exodus 34:7 that does seem to say that. It describes God as "forgiving iniquity, transgression and sin [but] visiting the iniquity of parents upon children and children's children." Coming as those words do on the heels of the assurance that God forgives iniquity, I am inclined to agree with those medieval and contemporary commentators who take those last words to refer not to divine punishment but the consequences of bad behavior on the part of less-than-ideal parents, causing their innocent children to suffer undeservedly.

A number of biblical passages emphasize that people are not held responsible for the misdeeds of their parents or their children but only for what they themselves do. For example:

> The person who sins, he alone shall die. A child shall not share the burden of a parent's guilt, nor shall the parent share the burden of a child's guilt. (Ezekiel 18:20)

> Parents shall not be put to death for children, nor children be put to death for parents; a person shall be put to death only for his own crime. (Deuteronomy 24:16)

My strongest objection to the theological teaching of inherited Original Sin, however, is that it seems to demand perfection of us, condemning us for anything short of perfection. I deem that an unrealistic, if not impossible, standard. A liberal Protestant minister of my acquaintance once tried to explain that doctrine to me in these words: "If I murder someone, that makes me a murderer, and I can't excuse myself by pointing to the billions of people I didn't murder. And if I sin, however trivial or inadvertent that sin may be in my eyes, that makes me a sinner, and I can't excuse my sin by pointing to all the sins I didn't commit." I told him in response that I didn't recognize the God he was describing as the God of the Bible. What kind of God creates fallible human beings, then sets an impossibly high standard of perfection for us and punishes us severely for not meeting that standard?

A crude analogy: I rely on my computer for a lot of things. I am using it to write this book, to send it chapter by chapter to my editor by e-mail, to make changes and corrections to it without having to retype the entire document as I did with my first book thirty-five years ago, and ultimately to transfer it in seconds onto a disc for publishing. In addition, it corrects my spelling. It enables me to send messages to friends and family anywhere in the world in seconds, something that took up to a week not that long ago. With my computer, I can access in seconds information that used to take me the better part of an hour to find. It is in many ways a remarkable machine, one I could not have imagined when I was growing up. But my computer has one exasperating flaw that I have trouble forgiving it for. It insists on perfection. It will not tolerate the smallest mistake. My mailman can come across a letter for me that misspells my name or gets my home address wrong by one or more numbers, and he will know that it is for me. I suspect if he had a letter addressed to "Natick rabbi who writes books," he would know where to deliver it. But if I try to send an e-mail to my brother, to whom I write often, and one letter is incorrect, or if I omit a space or put a comma where a period should be, the computer pretends it has no idea what I'm trying to do and rejects the communication entirely.

I resent being held to that standard of perfection. I'm only human. I don't want to believe that God is as much of a perfectionist as my computer. I can forgive mistakes made by my wife, my daughter, my grandchildren, my friends, and they forgive mistakes that I make with them, because we love one another and we know better than to expect perfection from a human being. Is God incapable of that level of forgiveness?

There was an unbearably sad story in the Boston newspaper recently. During the 2013–14 academic year, three teenagers, all of them excellent students from families who loved them, took their own lives for no apparent reason except perhaps the overwhelming fear of not being good enough. As near as anyone could tell, they were facing the pressure of getting into a good college. They were afraid that one B+ instead of an A would undermine their chances, and that their parents would see them, and they would see themselves, as failures if they had to settle for something less. I see that same sense of soul-destroying failure among gifted athletes who are almost, but not quite, good enough to play at the major league level, as they contend with saying good-bye to their lifelong dream.

Where did they, where do so many of us, get that feeling that if you're not the best, you're a failure? The God I believe in, the God I pray to, the God I turn to when I am at the point of losing faith in myself, is not a God who says, "I gave you one chance and you blew it. How can I ever trust you again?" The God I believe in says to me, "I have given you an incomparably valuable gift, the ability to know the difference between good and bad, between things that should be done and things that should not be done, the freedom no other creature has to use willpower to override temptation. And when you find that too hard to do, when you stumble and fall, when you are led astray by the pleasure of the moment rather than the long-term good, I will be there to pick you up, clean you off, and give you a fresh start, because I am a God of forgiveness, a God of second chances. Then when you are able to forgive yourself and to forgive people around you for not being perfect, I will recognize you as My child."

CHAPTER SIX

Religion Is What You Do, Not What You Believe

Every clergyman I know, myself included, has heard these words from a marginal congregant trying to justify his noninvolvement: "I may not be religious in the conventional sense, but I am a very spiritual person." The implication is that being spiritual, following a religion solely of the heart and mind, is a purer, more authentic way of communing with God than the physical act of attending church, giving charity, or performing good deeds. I never had a satisfactory reply to that claim until my friend and colleague Rabbi David Wolpe of Los Angeles shared his answer with me. He would tell his spiritual congregant, "No, spirituality is what you feel, theology is what you believe, religion is what you do." The most sublime religious faith becomes real only when it is translated into behavior, into doing things you might not otherwise do as an enactment of your religious faith.

The great Jewish theologian Martin Buber was once asked, "Where can I find God?" His answer: "God is not found in churches or synagogues. God is not found in holy books. God is not found in the hearts of the most fervent believer. *God is found between people*" (italics mine). When someone acts toward another person as his religious faith tells him to, God comes and bridges the gap between them. They are joined for those moments by bonds of holiness. The religion of your heart becomes real only when it is translated into action.

Many years ago, early in my tenure in my congregation, I had to officiate at the funeral of a woman who had spent a great deal of her life caring for a severely handicapped son, until his death in his twenties. She was in no way conventionally religious. She rarely attended synagogue services or any other temple activity. Caring for her son absorbed most of her time and energy. It would not be a stretch to say that that was her religion. If she ever thought about God at all (I never raised the subject with her), it would not surprise me if she resented God for not doing anything to alleviate her son's condition. Nonetheless, in my eulogy, I described her as having lived a life of holiness. "This is the fast I desire [on the Day of Atonement]—to break off every yoke, to share your bread with the hungry, to take the wretched into your home, and when you see the naked, to clothe them" (Isaiah 58:6–7).

A few years ago, the Reverend Lillian Daniel, a Congregational minister, wrote a delightful book titled *When "Spiritual but Not Religious" Is Not Enough* (2013). Early in the book, she describes a spiritual seeker who had tried out one flavor of Christian worship after another and found cause to reject them all. Now, he tells her, he spends Sunday morning reading *The New York Times* and gets more spiritual sustenance from that than from most church services. Then, he goes on, he puts on his running shoes and goes for a run in nature. "I'm one with the great outdoors. I find God there. And I realized that I am deeply spiritual but no longer religious." The Reverend Daniel comments in her book, "Like people who attend church wouldn't know that. . . . But push a little harder, on this self-developed religion, and you don't get much . . . depth," because "most self-developed Sunday-morning ritual has little room for sin," for an awareness of the wrongness of some things. It lacks a framework for understanding and responding to days, and lives, that are not full of sunshine and butterflies.

This disenchanted church abstainer tells her of how proud he is of his school-age son who wrote a report about children in faraway places whose lives are darkened by violence and hunger. The boy concluded, "It made me realize that we're so lucky to be living here and not there." The father brags that his son "really gets it. That's what our religion is, gratitude." Lillian Daniel responds in her book that "when you witness pain and declare yourself lucky, you have fallen way short of what Jesus would do. . . . I think God wants us to witness pain and suffering and, rather than feeling lucky, God wants us to feel angry and want to do something about it."

Her point, one among many, is that people who invoke simplistic reasons for rejecting traditional religion but find God in spring flowers and changing leaves will have no problem as long as it's sunny out, but they will have no framework for making sense of a hurricane or, for that matter, a business reversal or a diagnosis of serious illness. At times like that, you need a tradition to turn to that has seen it all and has no illusions about the world. You need a community, people who have learned to find God in the shadows as readily as in the sunshine, to find Him in the courage of afflicted people and the helpfulness of their neighbors. And you need people whose faith compels them not to pity you or to question God on your behalf, but to hold you and dry your tears.

Religion is like love. The difference between religion as feeling or believing and authentic religion as how you live out your faith is like the difference between love as a teenage girl's crush on her favorite pop singer and love as the relationship between a husband and wife who have shared years of good and bad experiences and know how to reach out to each other to gladden or to comfort. The first is a pleasant fantasy; the second is life-defining.

Readers of a certain age may remember an incident in the 1976 presidential election between the incumbent, Gerald Ford, and the Democratic challenger, Governor Jimmy Carter of Georgia. It was the first presidential election since Richard Nixon resigned the presidency in the wake of the Watergate scandal, revealing illegal and unethical behavior in the White House, and candidate Carter's Sunday school teacher piety was seen as a welcome contrast to Nixon's deviousness. But on at least one occasion, that piety misled him. He confessed to reporters after a campaign stop that he had "committed adultery in [his] heart" by noticing how attractive some of the women were in the crowds that greeted him. Someone might have reminded Carter how much the American economy depends on the billions of dollars women spend to make themselves look attractive. More than that, someone should have told him that thinking about something, even fantasizing about something, is not the same as actually doing it.

Old Jewish joke: The rabbi in his sermon points to a plaque of the Ten Commandments on the synagogue wall and says, "You see, according to the Torah, working on the Sabbath is exactly the same as committing adultery," at which point a congregant calls out, "I don't know about you, Rabbi, but I'm in a position to say they are not the same at all." Noticing how attractive a woman is is not a violation of the seventh commandment. Fantasizing about the prospect of getting to know her better is not adultery as long as you keep your hands to yourself. Yes, lustful thought can lead to improper behavior and can distract you from what you should be doing, but when it does, it is the behavior, not the thought, that is wrong. Only when thought leads to deed does your behavior cross the line, which is as it should be. We cannot always control our thoughts or our fantasies, but we have to learn to control our words and actions. In sin, as in religion, it is deeds that matter.

A correspondent once wrote to the advice columnist Ann Landers, "My husband is sixty-five years old, but he keeps staring at every attractive young woman in the street. How can I get him to stop?" She replied, "Don't worry about it. My dog chases buses, but he wouldn't know what to do with one if he ever caught it."

Some years ago, I was the Jewish representative on an interfaith panel of clergy. The moderator invited us to comment on the Seven Deadly Sins of Christian teaching. As you may remember, they are lust, gluttony, greed, sloth, anger, pride, and envy. The moderator solicited our comments as to which of the seven was the most harmful, which was the most common, and which was the hardest to avoid committing.

I heard my colleagues explain why each of these moral failings had the power to separate us from God and dilute the religious integrity of our lives. When my turn came, I began by saying that I didn't think any of those seven were the worst things a person could do. They wouldn't be at the top of my list of deadly sins. They might not make the top one hundred, because they all happen inside a person, not between one person and another, and have no impact on the real world until such time as thoughts are translated into deeds. My list of the worst offenses against God would begin with hurting another person, cheating another person, shaming another person. The Talmud characterizes causing another person's face to flush with embarrassment or anger as a form of bloodshed, a serious ethical violation. Sins—and, for that matter, virtues—refer to how we treat other people, not to what we think or feel in the privacy of our hearts. Only when those feelings are translated into action do they become part of our shared world.

I would say something similar about theology. Because I speak and write books about God's role in our lives, because I try to correct what I think of as unhelpful notions about God, I am often referred to as a theologian. I don't think that's what I am. I gave up any aspirations of being a theologian when I realized I could never keep straight the difference between ontological and epistemological proofs of God. My theology is less about who God is or what God does, and more about who we are and what we do because of what God means to us.

Beliefs, theological premises, don't qualify as religion until we translate them into behavior. Feeling sorry for a homeless person or feeling lucky that we have a roof over our heads, feeling outraged when we read of a crime or feeling lucky that we were not the victim doesn't help the homeless person or the crime victim until we translate those sentiments into helpful acts. For many years on the High Holy Days, I would share with my congregation excerpts from a meditation entitled "The Protester and the Prophet," credited to Robert Rowland. It read in part: "I was hungry and you formed a humanities club and discussed hunger. I was sick and you thanked God for your good health. I was lonely and you left me alone while you went to pray for me. You seem so holy, so close to God, but I'm still hungry, I'm still lonely and I'm still cold."

People are often surprised when I tell them, as I mentioned earlier, that there is no commandment in Judaism to believe in God. The first of the Ten Commandments—"I am the Lord your God who brought you out of the land of Egypt, the house of bondage, to be your God" (Exodus 20:2)—is not a command to believe in God. In fact, it is not a commandment at all. It is an introductory statement telling the Israelites assembled at the foot of Mount Sinai how they should live in response to God's giving them freedom. In Hebrew, the familiar passage is not called the Ten Commandments but *asseret ha-dibrot,* the Ten Utterances, the first of which explains why the assembled people should obey the subsequent precepts. There is no theology there, telling people what to believe. There is only religion, telling them how they should relate to each other because of what God has done for them.

T. M. Luhrmann, professor of anthropology at Stanford, made that point even more strongly in a column in *The New York Times* in May 2013. Professor Luhrmann wrote, "The role of belief in religion is greatly overstated, as anthropologists have long known." She cited one of my favorite authorities on the social function of religion, Émile Durkheim, whose grandfather was an Orthodox rabbi. Durkheim traveled to a remote South Sea island in the belief that the religion of the natives there, who lived a primitive lifestyle, would resemble religion in its earliest, most basic form. That assumption itself is somewhat primitive (people who don't have indoor plumbing must be living the way people lived and worshipped in ancient times), but Durkheim did come to some important and valid conclusions. He discovered that for the islanders, "religion arose as a way for social groups to experience themselves as groups." When a baby was born, people gathered to celebrate and to assist the new mother. What would a happy event feel like if you had nobody to share it with? When a hurricane threatened, people would work together to prepare for it and would assemble afterward to repair the damage.

In all likelihood, the primary role of religion in its earliest incarnation was to assure individuals that they were not alone in an uncertain world. When you have a happy event to celebrate or a sad event to heal from, you need to do it in the company of other people. Abstract faith, a religion of the heart and mind, religion as a private experience, won't do the job nearly as well.

It may well be the case that the word "religion" is related to the word "ligament," from the Latin *ligare*, "to connect." One might argue that the word refers to beliefs that connect a person to God, but I am inclined to side with Durkheim that the role of religion is to bind us to other people in order to evoke together the sense that God is in our midst. We don't go to church or synagogue to find God; God may indeed be more accessible in nature on a sunny day. We go to church or synagogue to find other worshippers who are looking for what we are looking for, and together we find it. We become something greater than our solitary selves.

It is a rule in Judaism that certain prayers, including the celebrating of God's majesty, the public reading of the Torah at services, and the newly bereaved mourner's affirmation of faith in spite of loss, can be recited only in the presence of a quorum of at least ten people. God's holiness is manifest not in a single person, however saintly, but among people who have come together to invoke the Divine Presence.

Human beings are at heart social creatures. I remember only one line from my yearlong anthropology course in college: "One chimpanzee cannot be a chimpanzee." I would say something similar about people: one person alone will never be a completely realized human being.

Some years ago, I read about a bizarre experiment carried out by some medieval king. He sought to discover what language Adam and Eve spoke when they had no one to learn language from. So he took several newborn infants and isolated them from all human contact to see what language would spontaneously emerge. I would have predicted that the babies would never learn to speak at all. The actual result was even worse. They all died. We need the fellowship of others to invoke our potential humanity.

Have you ever had the experience of watching a really funny movie alone at home or in a theater where you were one of only a handful of viewers? Years ago, I had that experience. There was a Monty Python movie that our son was eager to see. It had been playing for several weeks and was about to disappear from the theaters. I picked him up after school and took him to Cambridge, to a theater that specialized in foreign films for people with out-of-the-mainstream tastes. There were maybe three other people in the theater, and while the movie was funny enough, it was hard to fully enjoy it under the circumstances. That is why television sitcoms have laugh tracks—not to tell you when to laugh, but to create the illusion that you are part of a larger audience sharing the experience. That is why, although you see the ball game better on television with close-ups and instant replay, you *experience* the game better at the stadium, where at any moment one play can transform several thousand individuals into a single shouting, cheering organism.

My half century of experience as a congregational rabbi in a Boston suburb would endorse what Durkheim said about the role of religion in the lives of those South Sea islanders. I know from personal and vicarious experience the joy felt by a family planning a wedding or bar mitzvah celebration every time a response card arrives telling them that another of their invited guests will be pleased to attend. And at the other end of the emotional spectrum, I have seen and personally experienced how the single most effective way to ease the pain of the loss of a loved one is to have a houseful of friends holding your hand, drying your tears, and grieving with you. To me, that is religion in action. That is when religion becomes real.

One of the first pieces of advice I give to people going through a hard time—be it a death, a divorce, loss of a job, whatever shape misfortune may come in—is, "Please don't try to handle this alone. I know you may be uncomfortable asking for help. [This tends to be a problem particularly for men, who more often feel, in my experience, that asking for help is an admission of incompetence.] I know you don't like the idea of people seeing you at a time like this, when you are depressed and emotionally depleted. But a time like this is precisely when you need people to be with you. When you feel rejected by God, by fate, by significant people in your life, the best possible medicine is to be in the company of people who give you the message that you are a good, competent person and that they care about you."

Luhrmann goes even further in her *New York Times* article, arguing that belief, understood as agreeing with statements or propositions about God, is "an entirely modern phenomenon." She cites the prominent scholar of comparative religion Wilfred Cantwell Smith, who has observed that when the King James Bible was translated into English in 1611, "to believe" meant something like "to cherish, to hold dear." It may be related to the German verb *lieben,* "to love." Smith, and Luhrmann with him, suggests that the affirmation "I believe in God" did not originally mean "I am convinced that God exists," as if God were up for reelection and should appreciate our support. In Smith's formulation, it means something like "I care deeply about God, I pledge Him my heart and soul, I opt to live in loyalty to Him."

Think of it this way: When my first book was published and became a major best seller, the publisher sent me on an extensive book tour, taking me away from home from Sunday to Thursday for several weeks to promote my work. I can imagine people saying to my wife, "Do you ever worry about your husband spending all that time away from home surrounded by admirers?" And I like to think she would have told them, "No, because I believe in my husband."

In saying "I believe in my husband," she would not be affirming my existence; nobody would be questioning that. To say that you believe in a person is to say that you trust him, you can rely on him.

Similarly, to believe in God is not to affirm His existence. To believe in God means to trust God, to rely on God to be there for you when you are afflicted by despair, to light your path when you are uncertain as to what to do. Luhrmann wrote, "These days, I find it more helpful to think about faith as the questions people choose to focus on, rather than the propositions observers think they must hold."

Harvey Cox, the author of several widely read books, was for many years the most popular lecturer on Christian thought at Harvard Divinity School. His last book, written on the occasion of his retirement and published in 2009, is titled *The Future of Faith*. In it he confessed that he was worried about the future of Christianity. Cox suggested that Christianity began as "a movement of the spirit, animated by faith—by hope and confidence in the dawning of an era of *shalom* that Jesus had demonstrated." For nearly three centuries, the Age of Faith thrived. "Then, however, in a relatively short time, . . . what had begun as a vigorous popular movement curdled into a top-heavy edifice defined by obligatory beliefs enforced by a hierarchy."

Close to the end of the book, Cox offered this warning and prediction: "Christianity understood as a system of beliefs guarded and transmitted through a privileged religious institution by a clerical class is dying. Instead, today Christianity as a way of life shared in a vast variety of ways by a diverse global network of fellowships is arising." In those words, Cox shines a spotlight on the problem with a religious system defined by what a person believes.

Belief exists inside a person. As such, it has the power and the tendency to separate a person from his neighbors who believe differently. But authentic religion connects people rather than separates them into the elect and the misguided, the saved and those who walk in darkness. The primary function of religion, as Durkheim discovered and taught and as every congregational clergyman of any denomination has discovered for himself or herself, is to bring people together rather than to separate them, thereby increasing their joy and diluting their sorrows. For that to happen, one's theology has to escape from the prison of the self and translate into sacred deeds shared with others, deeds sanctified by having the fingerprints of God all over them.

CHAPTER SEVEN

Leave Room for Doubt and Anger in Your Religious Outlook

If you consider yourself a religiously committed person, if you think that your faith in God is an important part of who you are, is it ever acceptable for you to doubt God? Do you violate your own understanding of what it means to be a person of faith if sometimes you are not sure if there is a God or if you are not sure that God can be counted on to do the things you rely on Him to do? Can you permit yourself to wonder if the words and events attributed to God in the Bible actually happened, from the account of the Creation of the world in six days to the Red Sea splitting to let the Israelites cross as they left Egypt?

What if you are troubled by God's explicit condemnation of sex between two men (Leviticus 18:22) or the law that adulterers are to be stoned (Deuteronomy 22:22), let alone the ban on eating pork (Deuteronomy 14:8)? What about the demand that a man, who may already be married, marry his brother's widow should his brother die childless, and raise any resulting children as his brother's offspring (Deuteronomy 25:5–6)? Or the New Testament admonition that women should remain out of sight as much as possible and that their voices should not be heard in church (1 Timothy 2:11–12)?

If your religiously informed conscience is troubled by finding these passages in Scripture or in the teachings of your tradition, must you deaden your moral instincts and say to yourself, "If it's in the Bible, then I have to believe it is the will of God, and I have no choice but to accept it. I'm not going to set myself up as being more righteous than God"?

For that matter, is it morally and religiously acceptable to question the divine origin of the words of God, or even to question the very existence of God? As I have mentioned, my naive childhood faith in God was shaken by two events in my preteen and teenage years. I was ten when my best friend died of a brain tumor, and fourteen when the staggering extent of the Holocaust became known. I am sure I was not the only person to think, There can't be a God if things like this happen.

I believe it is not only permissible but a religious obligation to question the existence of God if you are troubled by some of the things you were taught, to question the divine origin of things that are said in God's name, and then to go on and search for answers to your questions. The only religiously unacceptable response is to reject religion entirely and close your mind to further speculation. I cannot believe that God would bless us with a critical intelligence, with the ability to extend the frontiers of knowledge and understanding when it comes to biology and psychology, and then say to us, "Stop, go no further" when it comes to theology. For me, the alternative to faith is not doubt but despair, the conclusion that we are alone in a cold and unreliable world.

The wisest answer I have found to the issue of the legitimacy of doubt comes from Anne Lamott, who wrote in *Plan B: Further Thoughts on Faith* (2005), "The opposite of faith is not doubt, but certainty." When someone says to me, "I don't just *believe* there is a God; I *know* there is," I am often tempted to respond, "In that case, you don't have religious faith; you have information." To me, faith in God is a lot like marriage, which is faith in another person. It means a rock-solid commitment to giving God the benefit of the doubt, not because God needs it (I'm pretty sure God could get along without us if He had to) but because we need it. I choose to believe in the reality of God not because logic demands it or because the arguments for it are persuasive, but because the things I do take on an additional dimension when I do. Joys become more significant and disappointments more bearable when I do.

In the same way that an intellectually honest scientist must be prepared to revise and, if necessary, discard his most cherished and widely accepted theories in the face of new information, lest he suffer the fate of those who cited Scripture to refute Copernicus, an intellectually honest man or woman of faith must be prepared to say, My faith in the reality and reliability of God is the cornerstone of my life, but I am prepared to admit that there are limits to my understanding of who God is and what He stands for. Should scientific or other irrefutable evidence of any sort conflict with biblical narratives or postbiblical teachings, I'll modify my understanding or acceptance of them accordingly. Because my tradition tells me that Truth is one of the names of God, I cannot in good faith maintain positions that conflict with Truth.

Can a religiously serious person doubt God's word, God's goodness, even God's existence, or does faith require that we suspend our critical faculties at the door of the church or synagogue? The Bible will remind us that some of the most faith-intoxicated people in history had their moments of doubting God's word. Jeremiah is the most personally revealing and most passionate of the biblical prophets. He brings the word of God to the people, as all of the prophets do (to be a prophet does not mean telling the future; it means telling the truth), but he is one of the few prophets who also talks back to God, challenging God, asking God why He has imposed on him, of all people, the unwelcome task of telling people things they will not want to hear. God's word to him is so stark, so condemnatory, that Jeremiah, who loves his people even as he loves his God, cannot bring himself to speak it. In his innermost soul he does not want to believe that these are the words of God, and he does not want to believe that God is commanding him to speak them: "For I bring evil from the north and great disaster . . . to make your land a desolation, your cities ruined" (Jeremiah 4:7).

Jeremiah hears other prophets promising the people that God will never abandon them, that He will work a miracle for them as He did for Moses, that He will never let harm come to Jerusalem or to the House to which His name is attached. Jeremiah asks God why he can't be commanded to deliver a message like that, so that people will love him. God's answer, in essence, is that this is what it means to be a prophet, to say things that you don't want to say and that people don't want to hear, but to say them because you cannot hide from the realization that they are God's truth.

There is a story, probably apocryphal, about a Roman Catholic priest who was troubled by the elevation to sainthood of a Renaissance pope who was a notorious fornicator and plunderer of the public purse. Asked if he didn't believe God had the power to utilize flawed instruments for His purposes, the priest replied, "It's not God's power I'm questioning, it's His taste."

Jeremiah is not the only example of a reluctant prophet who doubts God's taste in singling him out for the thankless task of being a spokesman for God, wondering if God might be making a mistake in calling him to prophesy. Any number of biblical personalities speculate that God may have mistaken them for someone more capable. Moses is not engaging in false modesty when he says to God, as cited earlier, "Who am I that I should go to Pharaoh?" (Exodus 3:11), and a few verses later, he begs God, "Please make someone else Your agent" (4:13).

In chapter 6 of the book of Judges, at a time when the Midianites were oppressing Israel, an angel of the Lord appears to a very ordinary farmer named Gideon and says to him, "The Lord is with you, valiant warrior" (6:12). Gideon answers the angel, "If the Lord is indeed with us, why has all this befallen us? Where are all the wondrous deeds of which our fathers have spoken?" (6:13). God has to perform a series of miracles in order to convince Gideon that it is indeed God calling him. The author of Psalm 44 begins by reminding God, "Our fathers have told us of the deeds You performed for them in days of old" (44:2). But today, he laments, "You have rejected and disgraced us, You made us retreat before our enemies. . . . You made us a byword among the nations, a laughingstock among the peoples" (44:10–14).

None of these biblical voices expresses doubt as to God's existence, His might, or His commitment to what is right and just. What they doubt is His availability in time of need (How long, O Lord, will You let the enemy prevail?) and His judgment (What makes You think I'm the right person for this mission?). They are all, despite their concerns, men (and occasionally women) of deep faith. Their example can teach us what it means to be a religiously serious person. It need not mean banishing all doubt. It means a readiness to live with doubt. It means giving God the benefit of the doubt, as we would for anyone we cared about, and in order to do that, there has to be doubt to begin with.

Doubts about God need not be seen as lapses of faith. They can be seen as manifestations of faith, concerns born of caring enough to be troubled by life's unevenness. In much the same way, anger at God for the unfair things that happen in life, anger at the world for all the unfairness that stains it, anger at what some people are permitted to get away with, need not be seen as a rejection of religious teaching. Anger, even anger at God, can be an authentic religious response. Think of that moment at the end of act I in *Fiddler on the Roof.* The celebration of the wedding of Tevye's eldest daughter is interrupted by a pogrom, an anti-Jewish riot by local troublemakers. They overturn the tables, make off with the food, and ruin many of the nicest gifts. Tevye's wordless response to the violations is not to meekly bow his head and accept God's inscrutable will. He shakes his fist at God in exasperation.

Several years ago, the summer camp that our grandchildren attended was struck by tragedy. The oldest campers had gone white-water rafting, as had been their custom at the beginning of every summer. It was an event those fifteen-year-olds looked forward to, the enjoyment of nature with a whiff of danger such as these young people never got during the school year. (Psychologists have learned that if you don't give adolescent males something slightly dangerous to do, they will invent risky behavior on their own.) There had never been a problem before, but on this summer day, one popular, well-loved boy stepped out of his boat and was swept away by an unusually strong current. He ended up wedged underwater beneath a large rock, and the best efforts of the adults involved could not free him. The entire camp went into shock and mourning. The director called me, as someone who had ties to the camp and had written a book about bad things happening to good people, and asked if I would come down to Georgia and speak to the grief-stricken campers and counselors. Of course, I agreed.

Adolescents respond to misfortune differently than adults or younger children do. Adults feel sad; adolescents feel angry. I am not sure where that difference comes from, whether from their newly discovered sense of vulnerability or the realization that what they have been taught at home and in Sunday school—that if you are good, God will protect you—is not true. I knew that before I could talk to them about my theological belief in a self-limiting God who does not control everything but gives us the ability to cope with life's unfairness, before I could tell them that I did not believe that what happened to Andrew was punishment for something he had done, lest they fear they had done similar things and would be the next to suffer, I would have to deal with that anger.

I asked them to open their Bibles to the beginning of the book of Deuteronomy, the last book of the Torah, and I showed them how Moses at the end of his life is driven to express his anger at God. He has served God faithfully for forty years, sacrificing his relationship with his wife and children on the altar of service as God's messenger, listening to the complaints of a perpetually unsatisfied people, commanding them to do things they might not have wanted to do, and forbidding them from doing things they might have been tempted to do. And what is his reward for forty years of faithful service? All those people who have made his life miserable will get to live in the Promised Land and he won't. Moses tells God He is being unfair and asks if He would please change His mind.

That seems so utterly out of character for Moses, who has served God so faithfully for so long. Why this outburst now, at the end of his life? My assumption had always been that by now Moses was a cranky old man, tired of holding in his frustration. But then I heard the Anglo-Israeli scholar Avivah Zornberg offer a provocative new interpretation. She suggested that Moses vents his anger toward God in order to give the Israelites permission, by his example, to give voice to their anger. He has heard them grumbling in their tents, expressing their unhappiness over having lived in the desert without permanent homes, complaining about the limited supply of food available to them.

Moses is astute enough to understand the risk of that suppressed anger poisoning the people's feelings toward God. So he, by his example, opens the door for them to express their feelings, which they promptly do. They immediately vent forty years of pent-up frustration. They complain that God must hate them and that is why He subjected them to all these wanderings. If God really loved them, He would have let them remain in Egypt and sent the Egyptians out into the desert. Then, shortly after giving the people permission to express their anger toward God and their taking advantage of that permission, Moses shares with them one of the most beloved verses in the entire Torah, Deuteronomy 6:5: "You shall love the Lord your God with all your heart, with all your soul, with all your might." The implication, as Professor Zornberg understands it, is that before the Israelites felt free to express their anger toward God without fearing that God would hold it against them, they could not love Him "with all their hearts." They would be withholding some of their most deeply held feelings. Their love for God would be halfhearted, an inadequate basis for a serious relationship.

I told the grieving young people at the summer camp, "I've come here today to do for you what Moses did for the Israelites in the Sinai desert: to give you permission to be angry at God. God is not going to do anything bad to you for being angry at Him. Do you know why not? Because God is on your side. He is just as angry, He is just as upset about what happened to Andrew as you and I are. God didn't make it happen. Why would God want to do that? That was nature, a deadly combination of wind, rocks, and water coming together at just the wrong time. What is God's role in this terrible story? His job is to give you the strength you may not have today but will need tomorrow, the strength to hold on to your faith in the goodness of life even now when you've learned just how fragile and unpredictable life can be. God wants to help you find the strength to comfort Andrew's family, to tell them how much he was loved." I quoted to them the words of a clergyman I know, a former college chaplain, whose son also died in a drowning accident: "I believe that when his car hit the water, God's heart was the first to break."

"You shall love the Lord your God with all your heart." If we are angry at God because of something that happened to us or because of something going on in the world, and we are reluctant to admit our anger either because it seems disrespectful or because we fear that God will punish us for being angry at Him, we won't be able to "love God with all our heart." We can only love Him halfheartedly. The wife who is afraid to tell her husband how bothered she is by some of his habits, for fear that he will be upset with her and perhaps even leave her, will not be able to love him wholeheartedly, and that inability will affect their relationship. The adolescent who is scolded for being angry at his parents "after all we've done for you," or whose hopes and dreams are mocked by his parents, will learn to keep his feelings to himself. That will be an impediment to his being able to love his parents as wholeheartedly as he would like to.

Accepting anger, ours and that of people close to us, has to be part of any honest relationship. If the opposite of faith is not doubt but despair, then the opposite of authentic love, wholehearted love, is not anger but pretense, censoring our feelings. I don't believe God is fooled by that, nor do I believe that is what He wants from us. God will accept our anger, justified or not, so that we can then go on to love Him "with all our heart, with all our soul, with all our might."

CHAPTER EIGHT

To Feel Better About Yourself, Find Someone to Help

"Rabbi, tell me why I should go on living." The woman who sat across from me and spoke those words was a member of my congregation, though I did not know her well. I had officiated at the bar mitzvah services of her two sons some twenty years earlier and had had no meaningful contact with the family since then. I would estimate her age to have been in the mid- to late fifties. There was nothing striking about her appearance or the way she was dressed. Her voice was flat, with little emotion apart from a pervasive sadness. Her husband sat with her, not close enough to reach out and take her hand. He seemed equally discouraged and did not say a word during our time together.

She went on: "There are no medical issues; my health is good. There are no financial problems. We put our boys through college at a state school and we can pay our bills. I had a job until a couple of years ago when I was laid off. It's just that I feel that most of the nice things that will ever happen to me have already happened and I have nothing to look forward to. I'm getting older. Neither of my boys has a serious girlfriend, but even if they did, and even if I approved of the girl and her family, I like to think I would enjoy going to their wedding, but then what? Two nice days in the next thirty years? And if I didn't get along with the girl's family, I wouldn't even have that."

I wasn't sure how to respond. My initial impression was that she was bored with her life, but I didn't think it would be helpful to tell her that. I have had conversations with people who had been seriously injured in automobile accidents and would never walk normally again. I have sat at the bedsides of people diagnosed with a degenerative disease that would only get worse. I have dried the tears of men and women (mostly women) whose mates had left them, their parting words being the prediction that no one would ever love them. And I tried to give them all reasons to wake up the next morning and look forward to the new day. But I had never before been asked to counsel someone who didn't want to go on living because she found life boring.

I began my response by telling her that I appreciated her coming in to see me. I told her I took that as an indication that she wanted help. "I can't believe you came here expecting me to tell you that I agreed with you, that life was pointless, so let me try to help you."

I pointed out that if her life was lacking in drama, it might be because she was operating with a limited cast of characters: herself, a husband, and two children. She had spoken about her husband and two sons, but were there no other family members, no friends, no organizations she belonged to? I thought she might consider reaching out to include a few more people in her life, and if she wasn't comfortable taking the first step to do that (I suspected she wasn't), there were all sorts of ready-made groups she could join. "I hope you realize," I told her, "that the synagogue isn't only a place where one comes to pray to God. There are a lot of activities—book groups, social groups, ways of being of service to the community—that don't involve a religious commitment, and they are always looking for new members." (The word "synagogue," the word "congregation," and the Hebrew term *"bet Knesset,"* all mean "a place where people come together.")

"The other thing that concerned me about what you said to me," I told her, "was that it was all about what other people were or were not doing for you, and that is something you don't have a lot of control over. I didn't hear anything about what you were doing with or for others, yet that might be the exact thing to start changing, the easiest way to feel better about your life.

"I've been a rabbi for a long time," I told her. "I've dealt with a lot of people who were hurting—women whose husbands had died or had left the marriage, people grieving the death of a child or the loss of a job, people whose deteriorating health left them unable to do the things they once enjoyed. In every case, I gave them one rule and it almost always worked: the best way to feel better about yourself is to find someone to help. The widow, the parent whose child has died or is critically ill, those people not only have the right, they have the almost magical power to say to someone else who is hurting something that doctors and clergy aren't in a position to say: 'I know what you're going through because I've been there. Let's talk about it.'"

The biblical book of Ruth, one of the loveliest books in the Bible, is a love story on several levels. It tells of how, during one of the periodic famines that afflicted the land of Israel, a wealthy man with his wife and two sons move from Israel to the neighboring land of Moab, where the famine is less severe. They live there for many years, in the course of which their two sons marry Moabite women. Years pass, the man and both his sons die, and the widow Naomi makes plans to return to the land of Israel. She urges her daughters-in-law to go back to their own families, and she will go back to her husband's family in Bethlehem.

One of the daughters-in-law, Orpah, says good-bye and leaves to rejoin her Moabite kin. The other, Ruth, pledges herself to stay by the side of her elderly mother-in-law rather than send her on the journey alone. She utters the memorable words used to this day by people converting to Judaism, "Wherever you go, I will go. Your people shall be my people, and your God my God" (Ruth 1:16).

(The names, as so often in Scripture, are significant. "Orpah" means "the back of the neck" and implies turning one's back on another person. Legend has it that, as a distinctive and unique name out of the Bible, it was supposed to be Oprah Winfrey's first name, but her father spelled it wrong on the birth certificate. The name Ruth, on the other hand, means "friendship, loyalty," and that will in fact characterize her.)

It is a very touching pledge, but when they reach Bethlehem and Naomi is greeted by neighbors she had known years earlier, she hardly seems grateful for Ruth's loyalty or her company. Naomi tells her old friends, "I went away full [that is, with a husband and children] and the Lord has sent me back empty." Empty? What about her daughter-in-law who has abandoned her homeland and her own family to be with her? I recognize Naomi's mind-set. I have seen it in my pastoral practice, in victims of misfortune or tragedy. They make it hard for me to help them because, on some level, they don't believe they deserve to be helped.

Naomi doesn't recognize that Ruth is there with her, even as she does not recognize what Ruth has given up to be with her because, at some level, she does not believe she deserves to be helped.

Perhaps following a theology I am all too familiar with, Naomi seems to believe that all these things have happened to her because she has done something to deserve them, and she won't let anyone help her. That attitude will change only when Naomi, in the next chapter, reaches out to help someone else. That act of thoughtfulness brings her to see herself as someone who can make a difference in someone's life and restores her sense of worth. As is so often true, helping someone else is the best cure for one's own sense of having no place in the world.

There is a similar story in the book of Genesis, one that we read in synagogue at High Holy Day services. The patriarch Abraham and his wife Sarah have been married for many years and are childless. Sarah prevails on Abraham to take their maid, Hagar, and use her as a surrogate. Any child she has with Abraham, they will adopt and raise as their own.

Hagar has a son, Ishmael. When Ishmael reaches his thirteenth birthday, Sarah remarkably finds herself pregnant and bears Abraham a son, whom they name Isaac. Now that Sarah is herself a mother, she resents the presence of Hagar and Ishmael in her home and prevails upon Abraham to banish them. He sends them into the wilderness with a day's supply of food and water. As soon as the food and water are gone, Ishmael cries that he is hungry and thirsty. An angel appears and tells Hagar to take Ishmael by the hand and lead him to a certain spot where there will be a well.

Most of the time when I comment on the story, I emphasize the point that the well was there all the time but Hagar was too depressed to notice it. For purposes of this discussion, however, I would focus on the angel's exact words to Hagar. The Hebrew in Genesis 21:18 is "*s'i et ha-na'ar v'hachaziki et yadech bo,*" usually translated as "pick up the child and hold him by the hand." But a literal translation of those words would read "make your hand strong in his." That is the Bible's prescription for finding one's way out of despair. Find someone else to help; find someone you can take by the hand and guide to a better place. You will not only help that person, you will help yourself. You will make yourself feel stronger by reaching out to someone else.

Helping another person is empowering. Think of it this way: If someone is in a bad way and you try to help him by giving him money, he will appreciate it but you will be left with fewer resources than you started with. But if you give that person the message that you care about him, if you listen sympathetically to his story instead of interrupting him and telling him what to do, you will be strengthening him even as you feel better about yourself.

There is a short story by the Russian writer Turgenev in which the narrator is approached by a beggar in the street. The beggar is disheveled, his clothes worn and tattered. He tells the narrator, "I haven't eaten for two days. Can you give me money for food?" The narrator tells him, "I'm sorry, my brother. Forgive me, but I have no money to give you." The beggar replies, "That's all right. You have given me something more precious than money. You called me Brother."

The late Dr. Sherwin Nuland first came to my attention in 1994 with his book *How We Die,* and I have followed his writings ever since. In his book *The Art of Aging* (2007), he writes about a letter he received from a seventy-three-year-old woman who was in many ways emotionally better off than the congregant who came to see me, but she posed a similar question: "When one has lived a full life with both happy and sad experiences and feels that the capacity of enjoying life is slowly slipping away due to old age, should not one end one's life?" She writes of how her hearing and her vision are fading, that walking is getting harder, and that she "feel[s] it is time [she] should die" rather than decline into senility and become a burden to others.

Dr. Nuland responds to her, making the point that there is more to life than the things we enjoy doing. "Sometimes . . . it is necessary that we live for others. . . . Live for the sake of those who love you, because they need you." Her loved ones' lives, he tells her, would be significantly poorer if she were not part of them.

He shares a personal memory of his grandmother when she was in her seventies and physically beginning to fade, and how much she was able to teach him in her final years. There were so many times in the course of his coming-of-age when he was confused, when he fastened on unworthy priorities, and his grandmother, drawing on wisdom born of years of both good and bad experiences, was able to set him straight. She taught him the difference between knowledge and wisdom. Knowledge refers to knowing how to do something; wisdom means knowing when and whether to do it. Dr. Nuland, graduate of a fine medical school, had plenty of knowledge, but he depended on his grandmother for wisdom. We will often take advice from grandparents more readily than from parents because we realize that listening to them doesn't compromise our independence, but also because at some level we understand how much it means to them to be needed and heeded.

The most readily available cure for the sense of despair that my congregant brought to my office was to instill in her the awareness that there are people and causes that depend on her, that will be better off because of her involvement with them, the awareness that the world would be a poorer place if she were not part of it.

I told the woman in my office, "You seem to be dismissing the prospect of your sons' marrying. You only spoke of enjoying or not enjoying their weddings.

But what about all the years that follow the wedding ceremony, the good times and the hard times of family life?" I was touched when I read the poignant words of a middle-aged Roman Catholic priest: "When I was young, celibacy meant not having sex. Now that I am older, celibacy means not having grandchildren."

There is a special bond between grandparents and grandchildren, and the woman in my office would be foolish to dismiss it. There is wisdom born of years of living that she will have earned the right to share. For the grandparent, there is the possibility of vicarious immortality. For the grandchild, there is love without the concomitant expectation of obedience. It is that rare and special love (I have been fortunate to experience it from both sides) that asks nothing in return.

"You came here," I told the woman in my office, "asking why you should go on living. I can't give you a compelling answer. I can only give you advice born of my own experience, which has probably been very different from yours. But I can tell you this with one hundred percent confidence: Stick with life, let more people into your life, learn to care about them. Leave them grateful for having known you. Cleave to your family, go to your sons' weddings. One day down the road, probably more than one, you will pause and remember this conversation and you will say to yourself, I'm glad I lived to see this. How could I ever have thought about missing out on this?"

I don't know how the story ended. I stepped down from my position as rabbi of the congregation not long after that, to concentrate on my writing. I never ran into the family at Sabbath services, nor did I read anything about that family's sons' marriages. But at least I didn't see the woman's name on an obituary page, so maybe our time together and my recommendation that she read Sherwin Nuland were helpful. If I were presented with the same challenge again, I would give the same answer. The best cure for feeling down on your own life is to reach out and help someone else. I've never known it to fail. And the best prescription for adding joy to your own life is to share your life with others. You will increase the happiness in your life by sharing their happy times in addition to your own.

For the mature person who can no longer find meaning and purpose in his life in ways he once did—perhaps he has retired from his job or done it for so long that the work has become mind-numbingly routine; perhaps his children have grown and have their own families— the best advice I can give him is: Go back and fill in the spaces you left blank along the way. Are there things you've always wanted to do that financial considerations or family obligations once prevented? Don't see your retirement years, your post-family-raising years, as enforced idleness. See them as the gift of freedom to live out the dreams you once dreamed but were forced by circumstances to set aside.

I know a man who, when he was young, admired his high school math teacher so much and did so well in her class that he thought he, too, would be a math teacher when he grew up. Those mathematical skills led him to an important and prestigious position as budget director for a large company, but he never forgot his adolescent dreams and the way one teacher made algebra exciting to a fifteen-year-old boy. Today in retirement, he tutors young people who find math difficult and teaches them to love math as he did. Then there is the woman whose children are grown, have married, and have moved out of state; she doesn't get to see them and their families as often as she would like. When she does see them, she spoils them terribly, of course. But in between, she volunteers as an aide at a local nursery school, keeping her grandparenting skills sharp on other people's children.

What they and others like them understood, what the woman who came to see me did not seem to understand, is that true satisfaction comes from what we do for others more than what others do for us. Doing for others lets us feel strong, competent. Having others do for us may be necessary at times and even gratifying. It can make us feel that we matter. But it runs the risk of defining us as dependent. It is not only more blessed to give than to receive, as the New Testament would tell us, it is also more empowering.

For the woman whose children are grown and who seeks to recapture that sense of purpose that parenting gave her, for the man who has either retired from his job or gotten to the point where it has become routine, for people who are looking to recapture that sense of meaning and purpose in their lives that work or parenthood once gave them, where does one start?

We start by opening our lives to let other people in—members of our church or synagogue, members of our book club or other fellowship group. Some years ago, Paul Tillich defined religion as what a person does with his solitude. He was paraphrasing something that William James wrote in his 1902 masterwork *The Varieties of Religious Experience:* "Religion . . . shall mean for us the feelings, acts, and experiences of individual men in their solitude." With all due respect to thinkers far greater than I am, I think they got it wrong. I believe we discover our humanity at its most profound not when we are alone but precisely in the company of seekers. That is why Judaism invented the idea of the minyan, the minimum number of people required to conduct a service. God's presence is more readily invoked when people come together. Our humanity is experienced at its best in the company of others.

Next, I would urge the seeker to open his or her heart to people in need. When we help others, we help ourselves more. Being able to help another person creates a good feeling that lasts well beyond the act of kindness itself. There are few better feelings in life than the knowledge that somebody somewhere is grateful we came into their lives just when they needed us.

There is one more dimension available to the person who wants to find life continually inspiring. I would tell that person to open his or her eyes to the beauty and wonder of the world. Too many people are inclined to think of religion as standing in opposition to the affirmation of nature. Finding divinity in nature, they claim, is what pagans do. Our faith, they insist, tells us to spend our weekend mornings indoors singing praises to God and God's world in a setting of artificial light, heat, and air-conditioning. I strenuously disagree.

As I have suggested earlier, it must be said that nature can be capricious, unreliable. Nature is not moral. "Good weather" is about our convenience, not the moral meaning of today's forecast. A beautiful landscape can be as deceptively beguiling as a handsome salesman. Yet nature has the capacity to stir something in our souls that touches on its divine origin.

I remember an incident when I was sixteen years old. I was a freshman at Columbia and had signed up for an evening class taught by Abraham Joshua Heschel at the Jewish Theological Seminary. One evening, Professor Heschel entered the classroom and said to us, "Something miraculous just happened as I was walking up Broadway on the way to class." That got our attention. We listened to hear what that miraculous event might have been. He went on, "Something miraculous happened. The sun set, and of all the people on Broadway, nobody noticed it except for a handful of observant Jews who got the message that it was time for the evening prayer."

Heschel was teaching us that a miracle need not be something extraordinary and inexplicable, something that seems to violate the normal order of things. The predictable regularity of the world, the fact that sunrise and sunset, the phases of the moon, the change of seasons happen with such precision that they can be anticipated down to the precise minute and never deviate, that is a miracle. The sun never rises late or sets early. (Joshua 10:12, where Joshua commands the sun to halt in its course until the Israelites complete the rout of their enemies, is not meant to be taken literally. It is a poetic way of hoping that the day will last long enough for the Israelites to finish their military effort. As Clarence Darrow pointed out in his 1925 defense of John Scopes for teaching evolution, had the sun actually stood still—that is, had the earth stopped rotating for even a minute, let alone several hours—every building on the planet would have collapsed, and there is no evidence of that occurring.) Even the exceptional events, the earthquake or the solar eclipse, follow strict laws of geology and meteorology.

The miracle to which Heschel was calling our attention was not that something strikingly unusual had occurred, but precisely that something utterly ordinary and predictable had occurred. A faith system attuned to the natural world celebrates the orderliness that makes our lives livable: sunrise and sunset, the change of seasons, water boiling at a predictable temperature. He was urging those of us who had come to take sunsets for granted to reclaim that sense of wonder, lest we live our lives in too narrow an emotional range. One of his basic teachings was that religion is born in a sense of wonder.

In the Jewish tradition, there are blessings praising God for the reliability of sunrise and sunset, blessings to be recited not when we speculate on the workings of the natural world but when we have actually experienced those moments. There is a blessing for the rainfall, even if it interferes with our plans for a picnic or a ball game. Without that rain, the crops would not grow.

I would tell the teachers in our religious school, "I don't want to hear that on the day of the first serious snowfall of winter, you called the children back from the window to return to page forty-three in the textbook. A young child's gasp of delight at the beauty of the snow will be as authentic a prayer, and as religiously grounded a response to the wonder and beauty of God's world, as anything in your lesson plan for that afternoon."

Heschel would lament the fact that so many of us live so much of our lives in such a narrow emotional range. He sought to remind us that joy, the joy of being alive in God's world, is as important a dimension of the religious life as piety and reverence. When you find no pleasure in success, reach for joy to wake up your soul. I remember how, a few years ago, an IBM computer defeated the reigning chess champion of the world. A scientist of my acquaintance said to me, "Doesn't that prove that we can create machines that are superior to people?" My response was, "Superior? What the computer did was impressive, but could a computer enjoy its victory the way a human chess champion would?"

Rabbi Arthur Green, a prolific writer on the spiritual dimensions of life, wrote in *Judaism's Ten Best Ideas: A Brief Guide for Seekers* (2014), "Beware of anything that threatens to take away your joy [in the name of religion]. In the end it will probably take you away from God as well." It is that capacity for joy, along with the capacity for love, for pity, for laughter, for imagining something that never was and summoning it into existence, that makes the human being special.

That conversation with the middle-aged woman who found life unsatisfying was memorable but frustrating, as evidenced by the fact that I can remember it so clearly so many years later. But in a sense, it was easier than it might have been. What if, instead of being a healthy woman who found her life boring, she had come to my office to tell me that she had been diagnosed with an incurable illness and that the next several years of her life would be marked by increasing discomfort and decreasing ability to continue doing the things she found meaningful? I hope that at a time like that, I would have been wise enough to talk less and listen more.

On an autumn morning in November 2014, an attractive thirty-year-old woman named Brittany Maynard and her husband left their apartment in Portland, Oregon, to keep an appointment with Brittany's doctor. It was the day he was going to help her die. The couple had recently moved to Portland from their home in Northern California so that Brittany, who was suffering from advanced and incurable brain cancer, would be able to take advantage of Oregon's assisted suicide law, which allows terminally ill people to choose when and how they die rather than let their disease make that determination for them. She chose to end her life before her illness robbed her of most of what she enjoyed and before her life became one of pain and diminished capacity. I have nothing but compassion for someone like Brittany, or the other 750 people who have made use of that law in the year since it was passed. But when a similar law was on the ballot a few years ago in my home state of Massachusetts, I not only voted against it, I spoke out against it and was relieved when it did not pass. I opposed physician-assisted suicide or a right-to-die law, not because I want people to suffer, not because I believe life and death are exclusively in God's hands (if I believed that, I would not only forgo all medicine, I would cross streets without checking the traffic lights). I opposed it because I was afraid it would make it too easy and too acceptable for people like the woman in my office, or the girl whose boyfriend has dropped her, to do something drastic when they are depressed and feeling hopeless, and find a doctor who would do what they begged him or her to. I was afraid that too many adolescents, too many single or divorced people, too many middle-aged men who had been laid off from their jobs would find life pointless and seek to give away their unlived years. Rather, I felt as I spoke out against the measure: let them find within themselves qualities of strength and courage they did not know they had until they needed them. There should be a legally and morally acceptable way out for someone like Brittany Maynard, whose courage and honesty I can only admire. But there should be a high barrier to using that way out.

That is why I was saddened recently to read the suggestion of a respected medical authority, Dr. Ezekiel Emanuel, chair of the Department of Medical Ethics and Health Policy at the University of Pennsylvania, that people decline all medical treatment once they reach the age of seventy-five and let nature take its course, rather than leave their families with memories of them as feeble, decrepit, mentally confused senior citizens. I am not sure how seriously he expected his suggestion to be taken, and I would be willing to wager that in seventeen years, when the fifty-eight-year-old Dr. Emanuel reaches the seventy-five-year milestone, he will find grounds for reconsideration. But I understand the point he was trying to make. Sooner or later, if illness or accident doesn't claim us first, the story of our lives will consist less of what we choose to do and more of what we need to do just to keep ourselves alive. As I write these lines, I am closing in on my eightieth birthday. I am still able to write another book, craft a sermon or lecture of quality, get to the gym three times a week, and enjoy the company of my wife, our daughter, and our college-aged grandchildren. But even as I write those words, I remind myself that I get tired a lot sooner and more often than I did just a few years ago. My appointment calendar will often list three or more medical appointments in a given week. I have cut back on driving at night and have given away many of my Red Sox tickets because the games run too late and going to the ballpark involves climbing too many steps. Despite all of that, I still think of myself as more fortunate than most. Feeble, decrepit, and mentally confused? Not me. But if it happens in the near future, I will depend on the goodwill of friends and family to lovingly put up with me and help me.

I will insist to my last day that life should be measured in three dimensions, not only length but breadth—how many other people does it reach out to embrace?—and depth—what values do I stand for, even in my somewhat diminished condition?

Rather than endorse Dr. Emanuel's suggestion that we essentially give up the struggle at age seventy-five and let nature take its course, I much prefer what Dr. Atul Gawande writes in his best-selling 2014 book *Being Mortal*. He insists that a person's last years should not be a betrayal of the values that his or her life stood for previously, even as the last act of a drama or the last chapter of a novel should build on what went before. But Gawande sees how often, in a misguided effort to keep elderly people alive at whatever cost to their emotional well-being and their families' involvement, "we condemn them to a life designed to be safe but empty of everything they cared about." In Dr. Gawande's words, "Our most cruel failure in how we treat the sick and the aged is the failure to recognize that they have priorities beyond merely being safe and living longer." Let them live boldly for as many years as they have remaining. Let them suffer pain and illness if necessary, rather than suffer loneliness and the loss of all that is familiar.

When the world-weary author of Ecclesiastes reaches the stage of no longer finding pleasure in life despite his wealth and his achievements, he discovers his remedy in these words: "Go eat your bread in gladness and drink your wine in joy, and your acts will be approved by God. . . . Enjoy happiness with someone you love all the fleeting days that have been granted you on this earth" (Ecclesiastes 9:7–9). The woman who came to see me that day because she found life boring and meaningless, the man who has trouble looking ahead to a life in which he will no longer be able to do the things by which he has always defined himself, might do well to ponder the advice that the author of Ecclesiastes came up with when he faced that question. I know of no better answer.

CHAPTER NINE

Give God the Benefit of the Doubt

When the United States was founded in 1776, it thought of itself as a Christian nation, by which it meant a Protestant nation. The constitutional ban on the establishment of religion probably meant that no one Protestant denomination would have official standing over others, unlike the case in many European countries. There was a substantial Roman Catholic population in several of the states, and there was never a question of their being fully accepted as American citizens. One of my favorite factoids of American history is that at the celebration of American independence in Philadelphia in July 1776, there was a massive outdoor party with food and drink, at which there was a section of kosher food so that Jewish citizens would feel fully recognized as members of the new nation.

This bit of theological self-understanding worked well enough until the 1840s, when famine in Ireland and violent clashes among the several principalities of

Italy as they moved toward unification sent an influx of Roman Catholics to these shores. Numerically, they did not change the demographics of the United States, and politically they had minimal impact, but psychologically they shook the foundations of our self-image as a tolerant Protestant nation. There were anti-Catholic riots, anti-Catholic discrimination in hiring ("No Irish Need Apply"), and, in rare instances, the setting on fire of Catholic convents. It would take decades for Catholics to achieve full acceptance, and even then the level of acceptance at the margins was incomplete. I was living in Lawton, Oklahoma, serving as a military chaplain at the local army post in 1960, when John F. Kennedy, a Roman Catholic, was elected president, and I remember the nervous jokes my neighbors were making, seeing Kennedy's election as the opening wedge of an effort to have the pope take control of American life.

But the conflict settled down, Protestant America came to understand that their Catholic neighbors were really a lot like them (it often boiled down to a question of which church you stayed home from on Sunday morning), and America came to see itself as a Christian nation, embracing its Protestant and Catholic citizens alike and writing Christmas and Easter observance into the calendar.

This self-image was next challenged in the years following the assassination of the czar of Russia in 1881. Riots and anti-Semitic pogroms throughout the early years of the twentieth century drove large numbers of Russian, Polish, and Lithuanian Jews (my parents and my wife's parents among them) to board ships for a new life in America. Again, these ethnic newcomers encountered obstacles to full acceptance.

If not as violent as the anti-Catholicism of the mid-nineteenth century, the discrimination was at least as intense and thorough, magnified by the fact that Eastern European Jews, unlike Irish immigrants, looked and dressed differently than their American neighbors and often did not speak English. There was discrimination in housing and discrimination in employment (the latter of which drove Jewish immigrants into lines of work where they could be their own bosses, leading to impressive success in such fields as retailing and the movie industry). There were limits to further immigration during the Depression, when there weren't enough jobs for people who were already here. The discrimination did not ease until after World War II, when young men from the farms and small towns of the Midwest served in the armed forces alongside young Jewish men from Brooklyn (every military unit in a World War II movie seemed to have a Jew from Brooklyn in it) and found that they were like everyone else. At that point, America's self-definition changed and we began to speak of ourselves as a "Judeo-Christian nation." There were prominent Jews in public office, on the Supreme Court, and in the upper echelons of higher education.

Then, as the twentieth century gave way to the twenty-first, we became aware of a sizable and growing Muslim population in our midst, increasingly assertive when it came to their religious needs (professional athletes playing while fasting during Ramadan) and political preferences (community positions on issues of Middle East politics have received particular attention). The self-definition of the United States as a Judeo-Christian nation left them out, and slowly but steadily, mainstream culture has tended toward greater inclusivity. First on the part of public spokesmen and then filtering down to the average person, American Christians and Jews are gradually learning to speak of themselves as "heirs of the Abrahamic tradition," since Christians, Jews, and Muslims all look back to Abraham as their spiritual founder.

This seemed like a solution that would please everyone except scholars of religion, who understood that each of the three monotheistic faiths read the same Scriptures and revered Abraham as they found him there, but each of them found a different Abraham in the pages of Genesis. Professor Jon Levenson of Harvard has written an excellent summary of the issue entitled *Inheriting Abraham: The Legacy of the Patriarch in Judaism, Christianity, and Islam* (2012). In it, he documents how the image of Abraham as presented in each of these traditions would scarcely be recognized by the other two.

Levenson quotes the Catholic theologian Karl-Josef Kuschel, who wrote, "Judaism, Christianity and Islam are three different religions, not simply three different confessions of Abraham." For Jews, Abraham is first and foremost an ancestor, the progenitor of a people living in the service of God. Theology is a distant second to peoplehood in the biblical account—believing is secondary to belonging. This perspective continues to this day. For Christians, Abraham is the believer par excellence, the pioneer of monotheism. In a world of idol worshippers, Abraham affirmed the existence of a single all-powerful deity. Paul refers to him as "the father of all who have faith" (Romans 4:11). For Muslims, Abraham is the symbol of unquestioning obedience, as exemplified by his readiness to sacrifice his beloved son (Isaac in the Hebrew Bible, Ishmael in the Quran) in response to God's demand.

That these three major religions have different notions of a proper relationship to God is not that surprising. What is remarkable is that all three base their theology, and their understanding of the role of Abraham in it, on a single sentence in the book of Genesis, a line that defies clear and definitive translation. The verse, Genesis 15:6, reads, "He [Abraham] [did something; the Hebrew is maddeningly ambivalent] to or for God, and He [God] reckoned it to him as meritorious." What did Abraham do to or for God, and why was God so favorably impressed by it? That is open to interpretation.

The Hebrew verb at the heart of the verse is *he'emin*. It is related to the word "Amen," which we generally don't translate but use in English to denote agreement or endorsement. Its Hebrew cognates include words that mean "trust" and "faithfulness." What it is taken to mean in Genesis 15 will usually reflect the theology of the translator, and the standard biblical translations vary accordingly.

The familiar King James Version (from the sixteenth century, contemporary with Shakespeare) reads, "He *believed in* the Lord [italics mine] and He counted it to him for righteousness." That is, the faith of Abraham was a matter of correct belief.

The Revised Standard Version, a 1953 Protestant-sponsored revision of the King James, offers us, "He believed the Lord [not: believed *in* the Lord] and He reckoned it to him as righteousness."

The first standard Jewish translation into English (1917, updated in 1946) largely follows the King James version with a few changes, reading, "He *believed in* the Eternal [italics mine] and He accounted it to him for righteousness." An update of that work, published in 1985, significantly amends it to read, "Because he *put his trust in* the Lord [italics mine], He reckoned it to his merit."

The Jerusalem Bible, produced by Roman Catholic scholars, introduces a new note: "Abraham put his faith in Yahweh, who counted this as making him justified."

The Reverend James Moffatt, a Protestant clergyman writing in the 1930s, whose approach can be summarized as "this may not be what the text says but this is what it means," rendered this fundamental verse "Abraham believed the Eternal, who counted his trust as real religion."

What, then, is this important but challenging passage trying to tell us? We learn that Abraham had positive feelings about God, not necessarily acted out in deeds, and that God was pleased by that. Does it make a difference if Abraham believed God or believed *in* God? I would suggest that it makes a significant difference. To believe in God is a statement about God, that He exists and is not the product of wishful thinking. It is theology more than behavior, and theology is something that exists inside an individual's heart and mind. To believe God is a statement about Abraham, that Abraham was prepared not just to affirm God's reality but to *trust* God, to rely on God to do what He had promised to do. For that reason, he was prepared to act in obedience to God's demands. Two of our translators, the Reverend Dr. Moffatt and the 1962 Jewish Publication Society version, specifically use the word "trust." Whereas theology exists inside a single individual, trusts exists between people. It presupposes a relationship. The verse then would be about God's nature as expressed in His acts. Abraham's faith was not so much in God's existence (there really is somebody up there) as in God's reliability, the confidence that He will do what He said He would do. Abraham took God at His word when God promised him that he would be the progenitor of an important people, even though Abraham and his wife were well along in years and had no children of their own.

My inclination is to follow that last reading. What Abraham affirmed, and what God commended him for, was not his faith that God existed but his faith that God's promises could be relied on. As I suggested in a previous chapter, when my wife affirms that she has faith in me, she is not just saying that I exist. She is saying that I can be relied on to do the right thing. Abraham did for God the one thing that God could not do for Himself. He gave God the benefit of the doubt. He trusted Him. Abraham's faith was the faith that what should be one day will be.

When I came to understand the verb at the heart of Genesis 15:6 to mean that Abraham trusted God to keep His promise and that God appreciated his doing that, I realized for the first time that this might be the key to understanding the single most enigmatic story in the entire Torah, Genesis 22: "Some time afterward, God put Abraham to the test. He said to him . . . 'Take your son, your favored son Isaac whom you love. Go with him to the land of Moriah and offer him up there as a sacrifice'" (verses 1–2).

Why is Abraham so ready to obey the command when it represents the destruction of his fondest dream?

I have read that story more than a hundred times and have never been comfortable with it. We read it publicly in the synagogue on the High Holy Days. I have consulted every commentary I could find, from the traditional view that God was testing the limits of Abraham's faith to the theory of Freud's disciple Theodor Reik that this was originally a version of an ancient society's coming-of-age ordeal, testing a young boy's courage by putting him through a life-threatening experience before he could be accepted as an adult. (In America, the contemporary equivalent would be high school football; among American Jews, it's called bar mitzvah.) I never found an interpretation that made sense of it or that left me able to admire either God for making the demand or Abraham for being so ready to obey it. When our son was mortally ill and some of my more traditional Jewish and Christian friends urged me to follow Abraham's example and accept God's decision that the child should die, I instinctively rebelled. I had no interest in serving a God who would ask that of his followers.

But as I ponder the meaning of *"he'emin"* in Genesis 15:6, for the first time I can see that story making sense. According to Genesis 15:6 in the interpretation I favor, the cornerstone of Abraham's faith was that he trusted God, not that he affirmed God's existence but that he affirmed God's reliability. God would do what He said He would do. Abraham trusted God to keep His promise to make him the progenitor of a great nation.

He was prepared to go ahead with the command to sacrifice Isaac *because he trusted God to keep that promise.* He relied on God to intervene at the last moment so that God's promise of progeny would not be thwarted, and that, of course, is exactly what happened. "An angel of the Lord called to him from heaven . . . and said, 'Do not raise your hand against the boy and do not harm him'" (Genesis 22:11–12). In a sense, Abraham was testing God even as God was testing him. Abraham is like the trapeze artist at the circus who has to be 100 percent confident that her partner will be there for her. Without that trust, the act can't work.

(Warning: Do not try this at home. Do not assume that God will never let anything bad happen to your family because you are good people. You're not Abraham, and God has not promised you anything like what He promised Abraham.)

This is what it means to give God the benefit of the doubt. It involves having a vision of the world not only as it is but as it can be, and believing that one day it will be. The faith of Abraham is a "theology of not-yet."

Thirty-five years ago, I began my first book with these words: "There is only one question which really matters: why do bad things happen to good people?" In this last chapter of this book, I would ask another, equally fundamental question: Can we trust the world? Is ours a world in which people can count on getting what they deserve? I look at the evidence and I can't say yes, but I refuse to say no, so I answer, "Not yet."

In the words of Rabbi Lord Jonathan Sacks, the recently retired chief rabbi of the Orthodox synagogues of the United Kingdom, in his book *A Letter in the Scroll* (2000), "Judaism begins not in wonder that the world is, but in protest that the world is not as it ought to be." The insistence that the world is not yet what God intended it to be is, to my mind, a more honest sort of faith than is an attitude of "if God made the world this way, with disease and crime and natural disasters, that must mean that He wants it this way until and unless He intervenes to change it."

Readers of a certain age may remember Robert F. Kennedy's paraphrase from George Bernard Shaw's *Back to Methuselah:* "Some people look at the world as it is and ask 'Why?' I look at the world as it might be and ask 'Why not?'" I would paraphrase the challenge to read, "Some people see the world as it is and say, 'I guess God wanted it this way, so all I can do is learn to live with it.' As an ancient proverb puts it, 'If you see a blind man, kick him. Why should you be kinder than God?' Others see the world as it is and ask, 'What kind of God would want this kind of world, with its wars, plagues, earthquakes, and all the other calamities that fill the pages of the newspapers every morning? A God who is comfortable with such things happening is not a God who can give me the courage to work for a new and better day.' "

The poet Archibald MacLeish, in his 1958 play *J.B.*, based on the biblical book of Job, puts these words into the mouth of one of his characters: "If God is God He is not good, / If God is good He is not God." That is, either God is incapable of making this a better, nicer world, in which case He is not the all-powerful Master of the Universe that we were raised to believe in. Or else He is capable of making the world better and chooses not to, in which case He is mighty but not all that good.

I would propose a third alternative to having to choose between a cruel God and a feeble one. It is what I call a theology of "not yet." It calls on us to see all that is wrong with the world as it is now but to refuse to accept that it has to be this way forever. There are forces striving to make the world a better place, and I see those forces as embodiments of God's will.

Had you been living in Spain in the fifteenth century, at a time when Spain was the most powerful nation in Europe, you would have had to deal with the Inquisition as an expression of religious and political authority, with people executed for "wrong" belief, and you might well have asked yourself, "Is this what religion stands for? Torture and death threats to make one believe? Isn't religion supposed to be about cultivating the divine attributes of kindness and reverence for life?" And the answer would have been, "Yes, absolutely, but not yet." In time, people would come to recognize that forced religion is not genuine religion, but it would take time for people to understand that. The human mind evolved slowly until it outgrew its approval of torture in the name of God.

Had you been living in Germany or in one of the countries occupied by the Nazis in the 1940s and had to witness the murders, concentration camps, and violations of the most basic rules of behavior, I suspect you might well have wondered, "Where are the freedom-loving, truth-loving nations of the world? Why aren't they doing something about this?" Ultimately, they did something about it, assembling the mightiest military force the world had ever seen, but not until millions of innocent people had suffered and died. Forces of hatred can do a great deal of harm before forces of goodness can muster the will to stand up to them.

I was born in 1935. As I grew up, my parents dreaded all the childhood diseases that could have affected my life and health—mumps, measles, chicken pox, polio. But my generation saw medical researchers refuse to accept the idea that these illnesses needed to threaten every new generation just because they had been part of the landscape of childhood for as long as anyone could remember, and one by one we learned to treat and then to prevent them. That is what a not-yet theology offers us.

Our son died of an ailment so rare that at any point

in time there may be fewer than two hundred people in the world afflicted by it. Yet there are doctors and medical researchers at this moment dedicating themselves to finding a treatment and cure. They refuse to say, "It affects so few children. Why can't we just learn to live with it?" Instead they say, "Those two hundred or so beautiful young souls deserve a chance to live and flourish. Who knows what wonderful things they may be capable of doing if we can grant them a normal life span? And who knows what other benefits a treatment for progeria can lead to?"

I am a rabbi. I visit people in hospitals. I officiate at funerals. I hold the hands of grieving sons and daughters, grieving spouses, grieving parents. I have an idea of how much pain and undeserved anguish there is in God's world. But as I write these lines, I compare the world around me to the world in which I grew up. Literacy is now nearly universal. Education is widely available, up to and including college and vocational training. People are living longer and leading more productive lives.

In 2005, on the occasion of the sixtieth anniversary of Franklin Roosevelt's death, I attended a gathering at which his memory was invoked. The chairman of the program shared with us a book that had recently been published about the Roosevelt administration, and he read from the appendix the names of some two dozen prominent figures from those years, including the years of their birth and death. Almost without exception, they were in their fifties or sixties when they died.

That was no more than two generations ago, and in two generations we have added almost twenty-five years to the average life span, and relatively few of the beneficiaries are spending their gift of twenty-five years of life in nursing homes or doctors' waiting rooms. I was recently invited to speak to a gathering of nonagenarians. You had to be at least ninety years old to be eligible for membership. There were about a hundred people in attendance, and when I finished speaking, they asked me some very perceptive questions.

Once upon a time, not all that long ago, the wish that a newborn child would live into his or her eighties or nineties might have sounded like a fantasy or a prediction of years of feeble confinement. But the response of "that's not possible" gradually evolved into a response of "not yet," and then into a common reality.

Abraham grew up in a world where religion meant worshipping idols. Religion meant seeking to bribe God to fulfill your request. By the time he died, religion had matured into an effort to learn God's will and live in harmony with it rather than instructing God how to run His world. Abraham grew up in a world where kings had supreme power over the lives and property of their subjects. Your Sunday school lessons probably skipped those episodes in Genesis 12, 20, and 26 where Abraham and Isaac feel forced to hand their wives over to the local king, lest he kill them and take the women for himself. Abraham's descendants today live in a world where, in most countries, governments are the free choice of the people, and where that is not the case, we say "not yet." Abraham grew up in a world where the strong dominated the weak and the weak had no recourse. That still happens in too many places today, but where it does, we no longer say, "That's human nature." We say that the time will come when that will seem as unacceptable as child sacrifice and the divine right of kings to take one's property. There is still work to do for a theology of "not yet."

God's gift to Abraham was the promise that his descendants would teach the world what it means to live in the presence of God. Abraham's reciprocal gift to God was that he believed Him. In spite of everything that argued to the contrary three thousand years ago, Abraham gave God the benefit of the doubt. That is what I take that crucial verse in Genesis to mean. He believed that what should be, but was not, one day would be. And because Abraham's lineal and spiritual descendants took up his implicit theology of "not yet," much of that vision has come about, and everywhere I look, people are striving to bring the rest of it into reality. This world is still not the world God intended it to be. Some human beings have made it worse and continue to do so, while others have made and are making it better. I am sustained by the words of Martin Luther King Jr., quoting

Theodore Parker, an abolitionist who died in 1860: "The arc of the moral universe is long but it bends toward justice." And it bends toward honesty and toward forgiveness and toward generosity. The heirs of Abraham, whether they identify themselves as Jews, Christians, or Muslims, honor Abraham's memory by sharing his faith that the world we live in is not yet what God meant it to be, and by working to bring about the day when what should be, will be.

A Love Letter to a World
That May or May Not Deserve It

Dear World,

We've been through a lot together over the past eight decades, you and I—marriages, births, deaths, fulfillment and disappointment, war and peace, good times and hard times. There were days when you were more generous to me than I could possibly have deserved. And there were days when you cheated me out of things I felt I was entitled to. There were days when you looked so achingly beautiful that I could hardly believe you were mine, and days when you broke my heart and reduced me to tears.

But with it all, I choose to love you. I love you, whether you deserve it or not (and how does one measure that?). I love you in part because you are the only world I have. I love you because I like who I am better when I do. But mostly I love you because loving you makes it easier for me to be grateful for today and hopeful about tomorrow. Love does that.

Faithfully yours,
Harold Kushner

Harold S. Kushner is rabbi laureate of Temple Israel in Natick, Massachusetts, having long served that congregation. He is best known as the author of *When Bad Things Happen to Good People*. In 1995, he was honored by the Christophers, a Roman Catholic organization, as one of the fifty people who have made the world a better place in the past half century, and in 1999, the national organization Religion in American Life honored him as their clergyman of the year.

A NOTE ON THE TYPE

This book was sent in Scala, a typeface designed by the Dutch designer Martin Majoor (b. 1960) in 1988 and released by the FontFont foundry in 1990. While designed as a fully modern family of fonts containing both a serif and a sans serif alphabet, Scala retains many refinements normally associated with traditional fonts.

Composed by North Market Street Graphics
Lancaster, Pennsylvania

Printed and bound by Berryville Graphics
Berryville, Virginia

Designed by Soonyoung Kwon